Toys You Can Build

TOYS YOU CAN BUILD

C. J. MAGINLEY

Illustrated by ELISABETH D. McKEE

Photographs by BILL JOLI

HAWTHORN BOOKS, INC.
Publishers
New York

Library of Congress Catalog Card Number: 73-10881
ISBN: 0-8015-7860-4

3 4 5 6 7 8 9 10

for
my grandsons
Kevin B. Seymour and Geoffrey M. Seymour

Contents

Preface

Good wooden toys are expensive and many times not readily available. That is one of the main reasons why this book has been written. I have designed and made toys for many years and the toys described herein are the result.

There is no reason why Industrial Arts classes in schools cannot make toys for nursery and kindergarten classes. Church groups, hobby clubs, parents and others with few tools can make sturdy, attractive toys by following the detailed instructions, illustrations and photographs in this book.

There is also a ready market for well-built wooden toys and a retired person, or one with extra time available, might well find toymaking a pleasant and profitable pastime.

Acknowledgments

To Elisabeth D. McKee: I want to give special thanks for her careful and accurate preparation of the illustrations and for all of the suggestions and assistance given me in writing this book.

To my wife Ruth: my thanks for her usually constructive criticisms and her unique ability to translate my penmanship into a readable manuscript with her typewriter.

To Lucille C. Landis and Robert P. Landis: I am indebted for the help given me when designing the ships.

Introduction

It has been said that "anything worth doing is worth doing well." This is certainly true when making a toy. The finished article should be such that the person who made it can look at it and be proud of his workmanship. The child who receives a toy made by one he may know and love will treasure it far more than a toy which has been mass-produced in a factory.

If the toymaker is to be proud of his creation he must sand all wooden parts carefully before and after they are assembled. Whether or not the toy is one in which he and the recipient can take pride will be determined in great part by how well this has been done.

A few suggestions for sanding might be in order as well as a few other things to remember when making one or more of the toys.

Sanding should always be done with the grain of the wood.

Finish sanding the toy with fine sandpaper. Production paper, while more expensive than common sandpaper, is very satisfactory for the sanding job.

Chamfer or smooth off all sharp edges of every toy.

Before starting work on a toy read the directions all the way through. Study the diagrams and photographs which supplement the printed instructions. The diagrams have been carefully planned to show the toymaker just how to construct each toy.

A try-square should always be used as a guide when drawing a straight line on the wood or when making sure that the edge of a piece is square.

A planer saw blade will give a smooth cut and is best for making toys. A blade of this type also saves a lot of sanding.

When making some of the toys it is a good plan to glue a part in place first to locate it, and then drive in the nails or screws.

The toy will look better if the nails are evenly spaced.

Be sure to locate nails or screws so that other nails or screws will not hit them.

If there is a rust deterrent on the nails, it can be removed by shaking or tumbling the nails in a can of sawdust. This will avoid getting fingerprints on the wood.

When using a screw eye the author puts a washer between the eye and the wood. Washers may be used in other places such as underneath the heads of pan or round head screws at the discretion of the toymaker.

While the directions for making the toys assume that power tools are available, many of them can be made with only hand tools. The power tools used by the author are a circular saw, belt sander, drill press and band saw.

When 1/4" plywood is used, birch or maple plywood is much better than fir plywood for toy making. Good pieces of plywood can often be obtained at a woodworking factory. Core plywood is excellent for the bottom pieces of many of the toys, as it will not shrink.

The author uses only a good grade of western pine without any knots for most of the parts of the toys. Basswood can also be used if available to the toymaker. Here again, visit a woodworking shop and you may find many pieces of good wood for your toys.

If the material in the thickness or width given in the material list is not available, pieces can be laminated to get the desired thickness or width.

The three dimensions for each piece in the supply lists give thickness first, then width and length last. The length is always measured along the grain of the wood.

When using a dowel, as with the hitches for the trailer trucks, squeeze the end or ends of the dowel with pliers to make indentations for the glue.

A white glue, of which there are many brands, is very good for toy-making.

When using glue, remember, do not use too much. A thin coat is better than a thick one.

A no. 28 drill is just the right size for the shank of a no. 6 screw, and a no. 18 drill is the right size for a no. 8 screw. Use a smaller drill, of course, for the pilot hole. Drill the pilot hole first and then enlarge part way for the shank of the screw.

The pilot holes for screws or screw hooks should be enlarged to a depth of 1/8" or so with a drill a little larger than the shank of the screw to avoid splintering the wood. It is also a good idea to enlarge the pilot holes for nails just large enough for the head to fit into the surface of the wood.

Ferrules can be purchased at a plumbing supply house or at a hardware store.

Several of the toys in the book are designed to use 1/4" metal rods for axles with Palnuts driven on to the ends of the axles. If Palnuts are not available, cap nuts can be purchased at some hardware stores. When Palnuts or caps are used, drive one of them on one end of the axle before inserting the axle through the wheel.

The length of the rod, which can be bought at a hardware store, may vary according to the thickness of the wheel or wheels from the length given in the list of materials. When measuring the rod, allow $1/4''$ for each Palnut plus the length of the axle holder and thickness of wheels and washers, to determine actual length of rod needed. If the rod is cut a little too long, add a washer or two.

Washers, between the wheel and the frame, will make rubber wheels run better. For $1/4''$ rods $1\ 1/2''$ fender washers are very good for this purpose.

If rods and Palnuts or cap nuts are not used, $2''$ no. 10 or no. 12 round head screws can be used for the front axle and $2\ 1/2''$ screws for the rear axle. When screws are used for axles instead of $1/4''$ rods, drill a pilot hole in the end grain of the axle holder $1/2''$ from the lower edge and centered.

Wheels, which may present a problem to some toymakers, can often be obtained from old toys which have outlived their usefulness. Then, too, wheels can be purchased at some hobby stores or craft supply houses.

Wheels can be cut out with a hole-saw, expansion bit or a band saw. Of course, if the toymaker has a lathe, or has a friend who has one, the wheel problem is solved more readily.

The hole through the center of the wheels should be large enough to allow the wheel to turn freely on the axle. If a little wax is put on the axle, the wheels will run much better. Or, the axles can be sprayed with silicone. This will prevent any squeaks. The author puts screw axles into a can with a cover, sprays silicone on them and shakes the can. This is a good method if several screws at a time are being prepared for axles.

While some of the toys in the photographs have rubber wheels, wooden wheels may be used instead on any of the toys.

The wheel diameters given are the approximate size most appropriate for the toy being described. Some substitutions will without doubt have to be made by some toymakers.

A good finish on the toy can be obtained by using a sealer and one or two coats of varnish. The toy should be sanded lightly with a very fine sandpaper between coats to give the toy a nice smooth finish. One of the urethane varnishes will be very satisfactory. If the toy is painted, use a non-toxic quick-drying enamel for good results.

The cabs for the trucks can be made according to the directions given with each toy or they can be made as follows:

Materials: Cab

4 pc 3/4″ stock in width and length specified in   A,B,C,D
     material list for the toy being made

Construction: Cab

1. Glue B to A.
2. Glue C to B.
3. Drive two 2″ no. 6 finishing nails or 2″ screws through C and B into A.
4. Glue and nail D to C.
5. Sand the assembled cab and round off the front and rear ends of piece A.
6. Install the headlights.

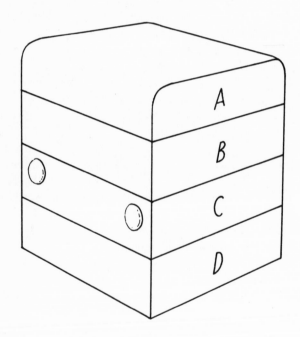

Toys You Can Build

Section 1

A Sports Car
A Hardtop or a Station Wagon
A Sedan and Two-wheel Trailer
A Station Wagon and Four-wheel Trailer
A Racer
Two-car Garage for Hardtop and Station Wagon
Two-car Garage with Overhead Door for Small Automobiles
Two-car Garage with Overhead Door for Large Automobiles
An Automobile Transport
A Jeep
A Bus

A SPORTS CAR

Materials:

1 pc 1 1/8″ x 2 1/8″ x 5 7/8″—A—body
1 pc 3/4″ x 2″ x 2 3/4″—B—top
5—1 1/4″ wheels
5—1 1/4″ no. 6 round head screws—axles
2 furniture nails—headlights

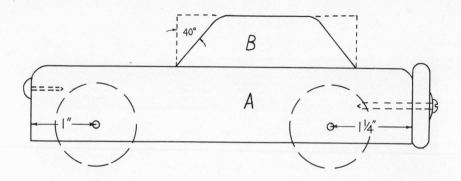

Construction:

1. Round off the top edges of the ends of the A piece.

2. Drill pilot holes for the axles 1/4″ up from the lower edge. The front holes are 1″ from the end while the back holes are 1 1/4″ from the end.

3. Saw the ends of the top at a 40 degree angle and the sides at a 5 degree angle and glue it to A.

4. Install the headlights and spare tire.

5. Apply the finish and mount the wheels.

Materials:

1 pc 1 1/8" x 2 1/8" x 5 7/8"—A—body

1 pc 3/4" x 2" x 2 3/4"—B—top (hardtop)

or

1 pc 3/4" x 2" x 3 3/4"—top (station wagon)

2 pc 3/16" x 3/8" x 2 1/4"—bumpers

4—1" wheels

4—1" no. 6 round head screws—axles

2—furniture nails—headlights

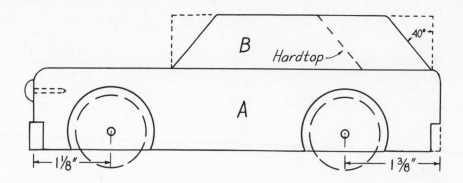

Construction:

1. With a 1 1/4" Greenlee or Forstner type bit make a cut about 3/16" in depth for the wheels. The center of each cut should be 1/4" from the lower side edge with the front one 1 1/8" from the end and the back one 1 3/8" from the end. Drill pilot holes in the center of each cut for the axles.

2. Make the cuts for the bumpers about 1/8" in depth and 3/8" wide.

3. Cut the ends of the top piece at a 40 degree angle and the sides at a 5 degree angle.

4. Glue piece B to piece A.

5. Install headlights and bumpers.

6. Apply the finish before mounting the wheels.

Materials: Sedan

1 pc 3/4" x 2 5/8" x 7 1/2"—A
1 pc 3/4" x 2 5/8" x 8 1/4"—B
1 pc 3/4" x 2 1/2" x 4"—C
2 pc 1/2" x 3/4" x 3"—bumpers
4 furniture nails—headlights
4—1 1/4" wheels
4—1 1/4" no. 8 round head screws—axles
2—2" no. 6 flat head screws
4 no. 6 finishing nails
1 no. 12 screw eye—hitch

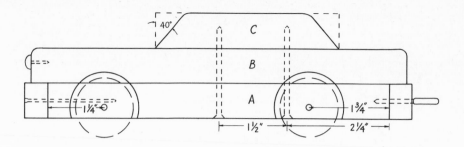

Construction: Sedan

1. Glue piece A to B allowing B to extend 3/8″ at each end.

2. With a 1 1/2″ Greenlee or Forstner type bit make a cut about 3/8″ in depth and 1/4″ from the lower edges of piece A for the wheels. Make the front cut 1 1/4″ from the end and the rear cut 1 3/4″ from the end. Drill pilot holes for the screw axles in the center of each cut.

3. Sand the pieces, rounding off the top edges of piece B.

4. Saw each end of the C piece at a 40 degree angle and the sides at a 5 degree angle. Round off slightly the top edges.

5. Locate the C piece on B and glue in place.

6. In the underside of the A piece drill and countersink pilot holes for the 2″ screws 2 1/4″ and 3 3/4″ from the back end and centered.

7. Install the headlights.

8. Drill two holes in each bumper for the no. 6 nails, 1″ from each end and 3/8″ from one edge. Also drill a hole for the screw eye (hitch) in the center of one bumper (rear). Round off the ends of the bumpers.

9. Glue and nail the bumpers to the ends of A.

10. Apply the finish and mount the wheels.

Materials: A Two-wheel Trailer

1 pc 7/16" x 2" x 3"—bottom
2 pc 7/16" x 2" x 2"—ends
2 pc 1/4" x 2" x 3 7/8"—sides
1 pc 7/16" x 3/4" x 2 1/2"—axle holder
2—1 1/4" wheels
2—1 1/4" no. 6 round head screws—axles
1 no. 12 ceiling hook ⎫
1 pc 7/16" x 7/16" x 2"—tongue ⎬ hitch
No. 16—1" brads

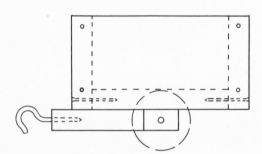

Construction: A Two-wheel Trailer

1. In each end piece drill a pilot hole for a brad 1/4" from one edge (lower) and 3/8" from the side edges.

2. In each corner of the side pieces drill pilot holes 1/4" in from the edges.

3. Drill pilot holes for the axles in the center of each end of the axle holder. Glue the axle holder to the underside of the bottom midway between the ends.

4. In one end of the tongue (front) drill a pilot hole for the ceiling hook. Glue the tongue to the underside of the trailer with the back end centered against the axle holder. Screw in the hook.

5. Apply the finish and mount the wheels.

Materials: Station Wagon

1 pc 3/4" x 2 5/8" x 7 1/2"—A
1 pc 3/4" x 2 5/8" x 8 1/4"—B
1 pc 3/4" x 2 1/2" x 5 1/2"—C
2 pc 1/2" x 3/4" x 3"—bumpers
4 furniture nails—headlights
4—1 1/4" wheels
4—1 1/4" no. 8 round head screws—axles
2—2" no. 6 flat head screws
4 no. 6 finishing nails
1 no. 12 screw eye—hitch

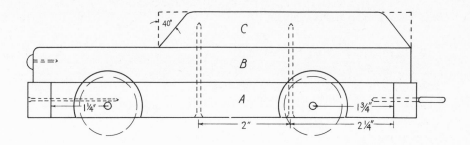

Construction: Station Wagon

1. Glue piece A to B allowing B to extend 3/8" at each end.
2. With a 1 1/2" Greenlee or Forstner type bit make a cut about 3/8" in depth and 1/4" from the lower edges of piece A for the wheels. Make the front cut 1 1/4" from the end and the rear cut 1 3/4" from the end. Drill pilot holes for the screw axles in the center of each cut.
3. Sand the pieces rounding off the top side edges and front edge of piece B.
4. Saw each end of the C piece at a 40 degree angle and the sides at a 5 degree angle. Round off slightly the top edges.
5. Locate the C piece on B and glue in place, even with back end of B.
6. In the underside of the A piece drill and countersink pilot holes for the 2" screws 2 1/4" and 4 1/4" from the back end and centered.
7. Install the headlights.
8. Drill two holes in each bumper for the no. 6 nails, 1" from each end and 3/8" from one edge. Also drill a hole for the screw eye (hitch) in the center of one bumper (rear). Round off the ends of the bumpers.
9. Glue and nail the bumpers to the ends of A.
10. Apply the finish and mount the wheels.

Materials: A Four-wheel Trailer

1 pc 7/16″ x 2″ x 4″—bottom
2 pc 7/16″ x 2 1/2″ x 2″—ends
2 pc 1/4″ x 2 1/2″ x 4 7/8″—sides
1 pc 1/4″ x 2 1/2″ x 4 7/8″ ⎫
1 pc 1/4″ x 1 15/16″ x 3 15/16″—A ⎬ roof (removable)
1 pc 7/16″ x 2 1/4″ x 2 1/2″—axle holder
4—1 1/4″ wheels

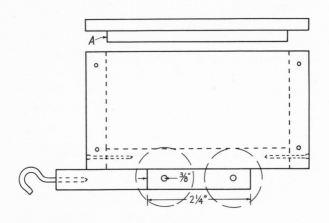

4—1 1/4″ no. 6 round head screws—axles
1 no. 12 ceiling hook ⎫
1 pc 7/16″ x 7/16″ x 2″—tongue ⎬ hitch
No. 16—1″ brads ⎭

Construction: A Four-wheel Trailer

1. In each end piece drill a pilot hole for a brad 1/4″ from one edge (lower) and 3/8″ from the side edges.
2. In each side piece drill a pilot hole 1/4″ in from the ends and 3/8″ from the upper and lower side edges. Also drill another hole 1/4″ from the lower side edge and centered.
3. Drill two pilot holes for the axles in each end of the axle holder 3/8″ from the side edges and centered on the end. Glue the axle holder to the bottom equidistant from the ends.
4. In one end of the tongue (front) drill a pilot hole for the ceiling

hook. Glue the tongue to the underside of the trailer with the back end centered against the axle holder. Screw in the hook.

5. Glue the A piece to the underside of the roof equidistant from the end and side edges.

6. Apply the finish and mount the wheels.

A RACER

Materials:

1 pc 1 1/8" x 1 1/4" x 5 7/8"—body
4—1 1/4" wheels
4—1 1/2" no. 8 round head screws—axles
8—3/16" ferrules—spacers
1 furniture nail—steering wheel

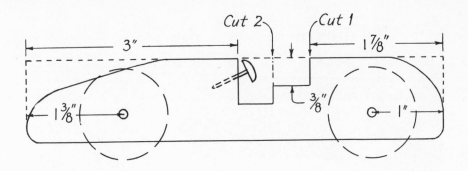

Construction:

1. With the dado saw make the 3/8" cut for the seat first. Then make the second cut 1/4" deeper than the first. See diagram. If a dado saw is not available make several cuts with the circular saw. To avoid any chipping from the saw cuts, the block may be a little wider than the finished racer and then cut to the 1 1/4" width.

2. Drill pilot holes for the screw axles 1" from the rear end, 1 3/8" from the front end, and 3/8" up from the lower edge.

3. Shape the ends of the racer on a vertical or circular sander.

4. Varnish or paint the racer. Decals or numerals from a calendar may be applied.

5. Mount the wheels putting the ferrules between the wheel and body. Ferrules can be purchased at a hardware store. Or, pieces of copper, plastic, or aluminum tubing can be used for spacers.

6. Install the steering wheel.

Materials:

2 pc 7/16″ x 3″ x 6 1/4″—sides
2 pc 1/4″ x 7/16″ x 3″—A
2 pc 1/4″ plywood 7″ x 8 3/4″—roof, floor
1 pc 1/4″ plywood 8 3/4″ x 3″—back
No. 18—1″ brads

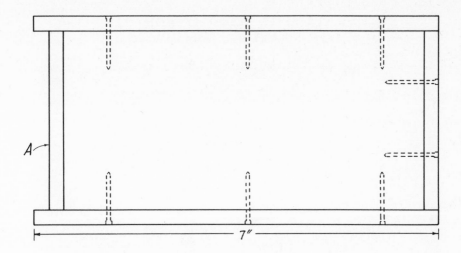

Construction:

1. Glue and nail the floor to the sides letting it extend 1/4″ at the back. It will extend 1/2″ at the front.
2. Glue and nail the back to the sides.
3. Put on the roof which will extend 1/2″ in front.
4. Glue the A pieces to the front end of the sides.
5. Apply the finish.

TWO-CAR GARAGE WITH OVERHEAD DOOR
FOR SMALL AUTOMOBILES

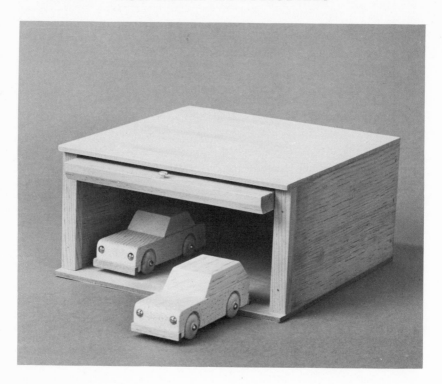

Materials: **Small Garage**

2 pc 3/4" x 4 3/4" x 8 3/4"—sides
1 pc 3/4" x 4 3/4" x 7 3/4"—back
1 pc 3/4" x 4 5/8" x 7 11/16"—door
2 pc 1/4" plywood 9 1/2" x 9 1/4"—floor, roof
2 pc 1/2" x 3/4" x 4 3/4"—A
2 pc 7/16" x 1" x 5"—stops
2 pc 7/16" x 3/4" x 2 3/4"—tracks
No. 6 finishing nails
No. 18—1" brads
1—1" no. 8 pan or round head screw—door handle

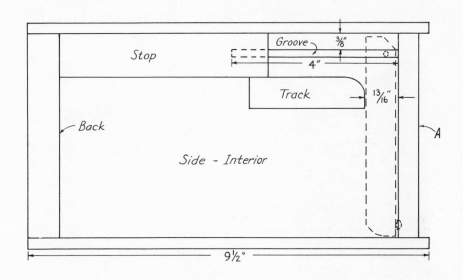

Stop   Groove $\frac{3}{8}''$

4"

Track $\frac{13}{16}''$

Back

A

Side - Interior

9½"

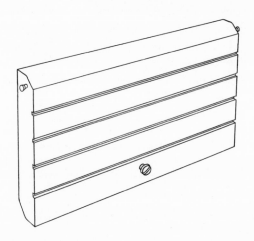

TWO-CAR GARAGE WITH OVERHEAD DOOR FOR LARGE AUTOMOBILES

Materials: **Large Garage**

2 pc 3/4" x 5 1/4" x 10 1/2"—sides
1 pc 3/4" x 5 1/4" x 9 3/4"—back
1 pc 3/4" x 5 1/8" x 9 11/16"—door
2 pc 1/4" plywood 11 1/2" x 11 1/4"—roof, floor
2 pc 1/2" x 3/4" x 5 1/4"—A
2 pc 7/16" x 1" x 6 1/4"—stop
2 pc 7/16" x 3/4" x 3 1/2"—tracks
No. 6 finishing nails
No. 18—1" brads
1—1" no. 8 pan or round head screw—door handle

Construction: For Both Garages

1. On the outside surface of each side piece drill three pilot holes for nails along one end (back) 3/8" from the edge. Locate a hole 3/4" from the top and bottom edges of the side with one midway between them.

2. On the inside surface of each side piece make a groove 3/8" down from the top edge and parallel to it. Make the groove 4" long, starting it at the front edge as in the diagram. Cut the groove 1/4" deep and just wide enough so that the head of a no. 6 finishing nail will slide easily in it.

3. Glue and nail the sides to the back with the grooves to the inside and front.

4. Nail on the floor which will extend in front about 3/4" beyond the sides.

5. Glue the stops to the inside of the sides, against the back and even with the upper edge of the sides. The front end of the stop will be over groove.

6. Round off one corner (top front) of the tracks and glue them to the inside 13/16" in from the front edge of the sides. The upper side of the tracks should be against the underside of the stops. See diagram.

7. Nail on the roof which will also extend in front. Be careful not to drive a nail into a groove. Space the brads evenly.

8. Make four horizontal saw cuts, evenly spaced about 1/8″ in depth in one side of the door to give it the appearance of an overhead door.

9. Round off the front upper edge of the door or cut the front corner off so that it will turn under the roof. Round off or saw off the lower inside corner also.

10. Drive a no. 6 finishing nail into each end of the door 3/8″ down and 1/2″ in from the inside edge. Allow the heads to extend about 1/4″.

11. Screw in the handle about 1/4″ from the lower outside edge of the door and centered.

12. Set the door in place with the nail heads in the grooves making sure that it works smoothly. A little wax will help.

13. Paint or varnish the garage, the door and the A pieces.

14. Glue and nail the A pieces to the ends of the sides. These pieces will cover the ends and hold the door in place.

Materials: Tractor

1 pc 1 1/8″ x 3″ x 8″—frame
1 pc 1 3/4″ x 2 7/8″ x 3″—A
1 pc 1 1/8″ x 2 7/8″ x 2 1/4″—B } cab and hood
2 pc 1 1/8″ x 1 1/8″ x 3″—axle holders
1 pc 1/2″ x 3/4″ x 4″—bumper (hardwood)
2 furniture nails—headlights
1 pc 1/4″ rod 4 7/8″ long—front axle
1 pc 1/4″ rod 5 7/8″ long—rear axle
4—1/4″ Palnuts
6—2 1/4″ or 2 3/8″ wheels
2—2″ no. 6 flat head screws
No. 6 finishing nails
(2″ and 2 1/2″ no. 10 screws may be used for axles instead of the rods
and Palnuts)

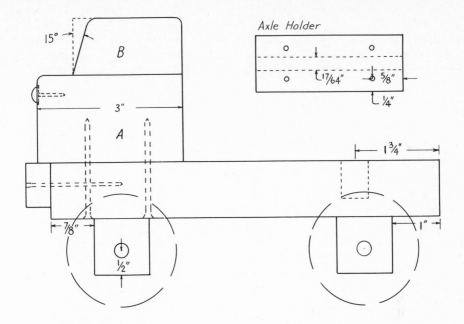

Axle Holder

Construction: Tractor

1. Sand the upper surface of the A piece and round off one top edge (front).

2. Saw one end of the B piece at a 15 degree angle. Round off the top front and back edges. Sand the front, top and back of this piece.

3. Glue B to A and sand the assembled cab. No. 8 finishing nails may be driven up through A into B.

4. Install the headlights. Shallow holes, slightly larger than the heads of the furniture nails being used, may be drilled so as to partially set the headlights into the end of the hood.

5. Drill a 9/16″ hole in the frame about 1 3/4″ from one end (back), about 3/4″ deep and centered.

6. In the underside of the frame drill and countersink two holes for screws 3/4″ and 2″ from the front end and centered. Then glue and screw the cab to the frame letting it extend over the front end about 1/4″.

7. Drill 17/64″ holes lengthwise through the axle holders 1/2″ from one side (lower) and centered. Drill four pilot holes for nails in the lower side of each holder 5/8″ from the ends and 1/4″ from the side edges.

8. Glue and nail the axle holders to the underside of the frame with the front one 7/8″ from the end and the rear one 1″ from the end.

9. Drill pilot holes for nails 1 1/4″ from the ends of the bumper and midway between the side edges. Round off the front corners of the bumper and glue and nail it to the frame.

10. Apply the finish before mounting the wheels.

1 pc 1 1/8" x 3 1/2" x 13"—body
2 pc 3/4" x 2" x 3 1/2"—front, rear ends
1 pc 7/16" x 1 3/4" x 1 5/8"—filler piece
1 pc 3/4" x 3" x 4"—axle holder support
1 pc 1 1/8" x 1 1/2" x 3"—axle holder
1 pc 1/4" rod 5 7/8" long—axle
2—1/4" Palnuts
4—2 1/4" or 2 3/8" wheels
1 pc 1/2" dowel 1" long—hitch
1 pc 1/4" dowel 1 5/8" long
2 pc 3/16" dowel 1/2" long
2—1 1/4" no. 6 flat head screws
2—1 1/2" no. 6 flat head screws
No. 6 finishing nails

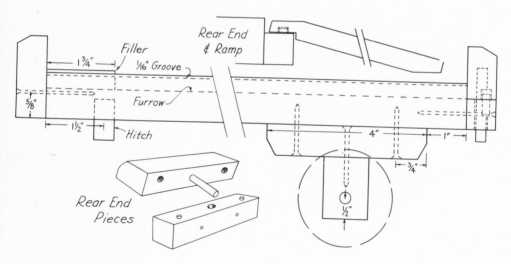

Construction: Trailer

1. With the dado saw cut a groove or furrow lengthwise and centered on the top surface of the body 3/8" in depth and 1 5/8" in width. A surface 15/16" wide will be left on either side of the groove. In each of these surfaces make a groove about 1/16" in depth and 3/8" in width 1/4" from each side edge of the body.

2. In underside of body drill a 1/2" hole about 1/2" deep 1 1/2" from one end (front) for the dowel hitch.

3. Saw the front upper edge of one end piece at a 30 degree angle. In this piece drill two holes for nails in the front surface 1/2" from the side edges and 5/8" from lower edge.

4. Glue and nail the front end to the body.

5. Glue the filler piece against the front end and to the bottom of the groove.

6. Make the back end as follows:

a. Drill a 1/4" hole 1 1/2" in depth in the center of the bottom or 3/4" surface. See diagram.

b. In the back surface drill two pilot holes for nails 1" in from side edges and 3/8" up from bottom edge.

c. Saw the upper back edge at a 30 degree angle same as the front end and sand the piece.

d. Saw the end lengthwise into two pieces, the lower one being 3/4" wide.

e. Enlarge the center hole in the lower piece so that a 1/4" dowel will fit in easily.

f. In the 3/4" surface of the lower piece drill two 3/16" holes about 3/8" deep 1/2" from the ends and 1/4" from back edge.

g. In the 3/4" surface of the upper part drill two 1/4" holes 1/2" from the ends, 1/4" from the back edge and about 1/4" deep. These holes will coincide with the 3/16" holes drilled in the lower piece.

h. Glue and nail the lower piece to the end of the body. Insert the two 3/16" dowels into the holes.

i. Insert and glue the 1/4" dowel into the center hole in the upper part. When the two pieces are put together, with the dowel in the center hole in the lower piece, the holes in the upper piece will fit over the 3/16" dowels. When the upper part is removed the ramps will hook over the dowel pegs.

7. In one side (lower) of the axle holder support drill and countersink two holes for screws 3/4" from front and rear edges and equidistant from side edges. In the upper surface of the axle holder support drill and countersink two holes for 1 1/2" screws 3/4" from side edges and centered. Saw the lower front and rear edges of the holder at 30 degree angles. See diagram.

8. Drill a 17/64" hole lengthwise through the axle holder 1/2" from one side (lower) and centered. Glue the axle holder to the support midway between the ends. Drive the 1 1/2" screws through the support into the axle holder.

9. Glue and screw the axle holder assembly to the body 1" from the back end.

10. Glue the hitch in the hole.

11. Apply the finish before mounting the wheels.

Materials: **Ramps**

2 pc 1/2" x 3/4" x 11"

Construction: **Ramps**

1. At one end of the ramp, using the two saws and chippers, make a crosscut with the dado saw tilted at 15 degrees. The cut should be 5/8" to 11/16" wide and 3/16" deep.

2. Make cut 2 the same way at the other end.

3. Turn the piece over so that the end where cut 1 was made is to the left and make cut 3.

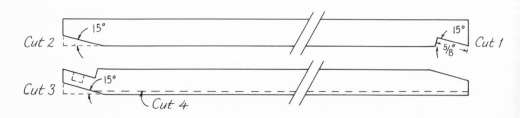

4. Remove all of the chippers except one and, with the dado saw in the normal position, make a groove about 3/8" wide and 1/16" deep lengthwise through the center of the 3/4" surface opposite the surface where cut 1 was made.

5. Drill a 7/32" hole about 1/8" deep in the center of cut 1. This hole will fit over the 3/16" dowel in the back of the trailer, when the ramp is being used.

If a dado saw is not available, the ends can be shaped with hand tools and the groove made by making several cuts with the circular saw.

Materials: **Automobiles for the Transport**

2 pc 1 1/8" x 2 1/8" x 6 1/8"—body
2 pc 3/4" x 2" x 2 3/4"—top
8—1 1/4" wheels
8—1 1/4" no. 6 round head screws
4—furniture nails—headlights

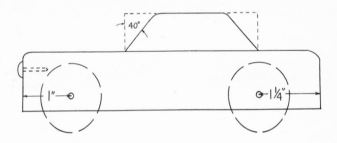

Construction: **Automobiles for the Transport**

1. Round off the top front and rear ends of the body.
2. Drill pilot holes for the axles 1/4" from the lower side edges. Locate the front holes 1" from the end and the rear holes 1 1/4" from the end.
3. Saw the ends of the top at 40 degree angles, and the sides at 5 degree angles.
4. Glue the top to the body.
5. Install the headlights.
6. Apply the finish before mounting the wheels.

A JEEP

Materials:

1 pc 7/16″ x 3 1/2″ x 8 1/16″—frame
1 pc 7/16″ x 1 1/2″ x 3 1/2″—back end
1 pc 7/16″ x 1 7/8″ x 3 1/2″—dashboard
2 pc 7/16″ x 1 1/2″ x 8 1/2″—for fenders
1 pc 7/16″ x 1/2″ x 4″—bumper (hardwood is best)
2 pc 3/4″ x 3 1/2″ x 3″—hood
2 pc 3/4″ x 1 1/2″ x 1″. ⎫
2 pc 7/16″ x 1 1/2″ x 1 5/8″—back ⎬ front seats
2 pc 3/4″ x 7/8″ x 2 1/4″—side seats
2 pc 7/16″ x 1 1/4″ x 3 1/2″—axle holders
2—1/4″ rods 5″ long—axles
4—1/4″ Palnuts
5—2″ wheels
1—1″ wheel—steering wheel
2—3/16″ ferrules—spacers
1—1 1/2″ no. 6 round head screw—steering post
1—3/4″ no. 6 round head screw—spare wheel
No. 16 or 18 brads 1 1/4″ long
2—no. 4 finishing nails—for bumper

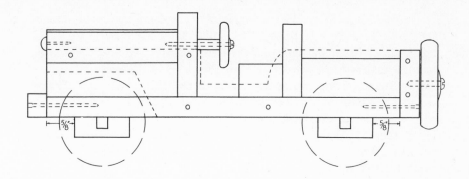

Construction:

1. Make the hood by gluing the two pieces together. Then shape as shown by making a thin saw cut (about 1/16"), 1" in depth along each side edge of the hood. Use a planer saw, if possible, as it will give a smoother cut. Then, round off the side edges on the sander or with a molding cutter.

2. Drive in the headlights.

3. Glue the hood to the front end of the frame.

4. Glue and nail the back piece to the frame.

5. Saw out the fenders using the diagram as a guide. Round off the top corners at the front and rear ends. Glue and nail the fenders to the hood, frame and end piece.

6. Glue the side seats to the floor and fenders with 3/4" surface on the floor.

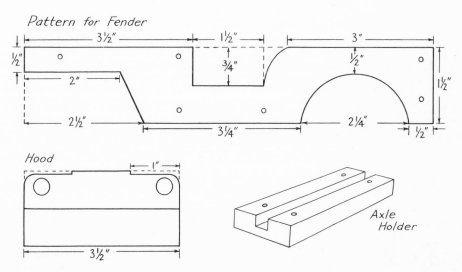

Pattern for Fender

Hood

Axle Holder

7. Make a groove 9/32" wide and 9/32" in depth lengthwise through the center of each axle holder. Drill pilot holes for nails in each axle holder 1/2" from the ends and 1/4" from the side edges. Glue and nail the holders to the frame 5/8" from the ends of the frame.

8. Round off the two upper corners of the dash. Drill a no. 28 hole through the dash 5/8" from the upper edge and 3/4" from one side edge (left—when installed).

9. Glue the dash to the end of the hood. Install the steering wheel using the ferrules or a short piece of tubing on the steering post as a spacer between the wheel and dashboard.

10. Make the front seats rounding off top edges, and glue them in place.

11. Fasten the bumper to the front end of the frame.

12. Apply the finish.

13. Mount the wheels. Screw the spare wheel to the back using the 3/4" screw.

A BUS

Materials:

1 pc 3/4″ x 3 1/2″ x 11 3/4″—bottom
2 pc 3/4″ x 3 1/2″ x 3 1/4″—ends
2 pc 7/16″ x 2 1/8″ x 11 3/4″—A ⎫
2 pc 7/16″ x 7/8″ x 11 3/4″—B ⎬ sides
2 pc 3/4″ x 4 1/2″ x 4″—front, rear pieces
1 pc 7/16″ x 4 3/8″ x 13 1/4″—roof
1 pc 1/4″ x 3 7/16″ x 10 3/16″—C
2 pc 1/2″ x 3/4″ x 4 3/4″—bumpers
2 furniture nails—headlights
2 pc 1/8″ plastic 1 1/4″ x 12″—windows
2—1 1/4″ no. 6 flat head screws
4—2″ wheels
4—1 1/2″ no. 8 round head screws—axles
No. 6 finishing nails
No. 4 finishing nails

Construction:

1. In each end piece drill and countersink a hole for a screw 3/4" from the upper edge and centered.

2. At each end of the bottom drill three pilot holes 1/2" in from the end and evenly spaced for the no. 6 nails.

3. Glue and nail the bottom to the ends.

4. With a 2 1/4" Greenlee or Forstner type bit cut openings about 5/16" in depth for the wheels in the lower edges of side sections A, 2" from the ends and 3/8" from the lower edges.

5. In the upper edge of each A piece saw a groove slightly wider than the thickness of the plastic windows and about 1/8" in depth. Cut the same size groove in the lower edge of each B piece.

6. At each corner of the side pieces A, drill a pilot hole for a no. 4 nail 3/8" in from the edges. In side piece B also drill a hole at each end 3/8" from the edge and midway between the side edges.

7. Glue and nail the sides to the ends and bottom.

8. Drill pilot holes for the screw axles through the center of each of the 2 1/4" holes and into the edges of the bottom of the bus.

9. Round off the side edges of the front and rear pieces with the sander or molding cutter. On the inside surface of these pieces saw grooves lengthwise about 3/16" wide, 1/8" in depth and 1/8" in from the side edges for the windows to fit into. Also cut out a piece 3/4" wide and 3/8" deep in the lower outside edge of the front and rear sections for the bumpers.

10. Drive the headlights into the front piece about 3/4" above the groove for the bumper.

11. Drill holes for no. 6 nails 1 1/2" from either end of the bumpers. Round off the front ends of the bumpers and glue them in the grooves sawed out for them.

12. Glue the front piece to the end even with the upper edge of the end. Drive a screw from the inside of the bus through the end into the front piece. Nail the bumper in place.

13. Round off the side edges of the roof and also the corners to conform to the rounded corners of the front and rear pieces. (The rear piece may be temporarily screwed in place for this and then removed.)

14. Glue the C piece to the underside of the roof 1 1/2" from one end and equidistant from the side edges.

15. Varnish or paint the bus at this point.

16. Install the windows.

17. Glue and screw the back piece on.

18. Install the rear bumper.

19. Mount the wheels.

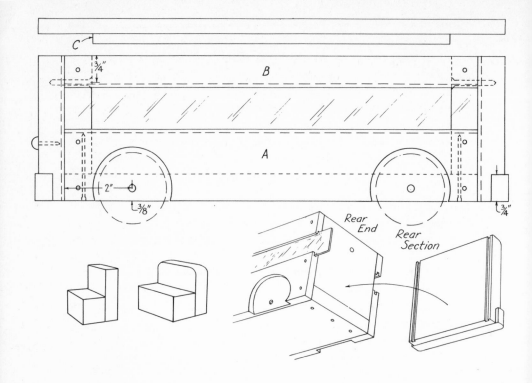

Seats and a steering wheel may be installed in the bus. If so, the following materials will be needed:

1 pc 3/4″ x 1″ x 3/4″
1 pc 3/8″ x 1″ x 1 1/2″—back } driver's seat

8 pc 3/4″ x 1 3/8″ x 3/4″
8 pc 3/8″ x 1 3/8″ x 1 1/2″—backs } passenger seats

1—1 1/4″ no. 6 pan or round head screw
1—1″ wheel
2—3/16″ ferrules—spacers
   (or 1/2″ pc of tubing) } steering wheel assembly

Construction:

1. Round off two corners (upper) of the seat backs. Glue the seats to the backs even with the lower ends of the backs.

2. Glue the passenger seats along each side spaced about 7/8″ apart.

3. Punch a pilot hole at a slight downward angle for the steering wheel shaft in the front end 1″ above the floor and 3/4″ from the left side. Install the steering wheel.

4. Glue the driver's seat in place behind the steering wheel.

54

Section 2

A Pick-up Truck
A Delivery Truck
A Small Van Trailer Truck
A Small Open Trailer Truck
A Small Flatbed Trailer Truck

A PICK-UP TRUCK

Materials:

1 pc 3/4" x 3" x 8"—frame
1 pc 3/4" x 3" x 2 3/4"—A ⎫
1 pc 1 1/8" x 3" x 2 3/4"—B ⎬ cab
1 pc 1 1/8" x 3" x 2 3/4"—C ⎭
2 pc 7/8" x 1 1/8" x 3"—axle holders
1 pc 1/2" x 3/4" x 4"—bumper (hardwood)
1 pc 3/4" x 3 1/2" x 5 3/8"—bottom ⎫
2 pc 7/16" x 2 1/4" x 6 1/4"—sides ⎬ box
2 pc 7/16" x 2 1/4" x 3 1/2"—ends ⎭
2 furniture nails—headlights
2—2" no. 10 screws—front axles
2—2 1/2" no. 10 screws—rear axles
2—1 1/4" no. 6 flat head screws
2—1 1/2" no. 6 flat head screws
No. 4 finishing nails
No. 6 finishing nails
6—2" wheels

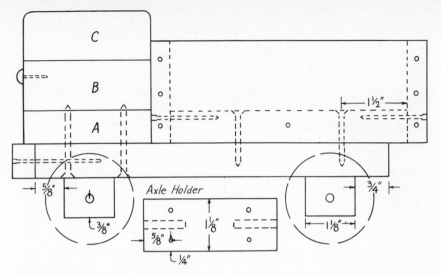

Axle Holder

Construction:

1. Glue and nail B to C and then A to B.

2. Sand the cab rounding off the top front and back edges of the C piece.

3. Drive in the headlights.

4. In the underside of the frame drill and countersink two holes for 1 1/2" screws 3/4" and 2″ from the front end and centered. Glue and screw the cab to the frame letting it extend over the front end about 1/4".

5. Drill pilot holes for no. 6 nails 1 1/4" in from the ends of the bumper and centered. Round off the front ends of the bumper and glue and nail it to the front end of the frame.

6. In the ends of each axle holder drill a pilot hole for the axles 3/8" from the lower edge and centered. In the 1 1/8" wide surface, locate the four pilot holes for the no. 4 nails 5/8" from the ends and 1/4" from the side edges.

7. Glue and nail the axle holders to the underside of the frame with the front holder 5/8" from the end and the rear one 3/4" from the end.

8. In the upper side of the bottom of the box drill and countersink holes 1 1/2" from either end and centered for the 1 1/4" screws.

9. In each corner of the side pieces, drill a pilot hole for the no. 4 nails 1/4" from the front and back edges and 3/8" from the top and bottom edges. Also, drill a hole midway between these holes at the front, back and bottom edges.

10. In the end pieces drill pilot holes for nails 3/4" from the side edges and 1/2" from the lower edge.

11. Glue and nail the ends to the bottom and the sides to the ends and bottom.

12. Apply the finish to the box, frame and cab.

13. Glue and screw the box to the frame.

14. Mount the wheels.

A DELIVERY TRUCK

Materials:

1 pc 3/4" x 3" x 8"—frame
1 pc 3/4" x 3" x 2 3/4"—A ⎤
1 pc 1 1/8" x 3" x 2 3/4"—B ⎬ cab
1 pc 1 1/8" x 3" x 2 3/4"—C ⎦
2 pc 7/8" x 1 1/8" x 3"—axle holders
1 pc 1/2" x 3/4" x 4"—bumper (hardwood)
1 pc 3/4" x 3 1/2" x 5 3/8"—bottom ⎤
2 pc 7/16" x 3 1/2" x 6 1/4"—sides ⎬ box
2 pc 7/16" x 3 1/2" x 3 1/2"—ends ⎦
1 pc 1/4" plywood 4 3/8" x 6 1/4"—D ⎤ roof (removable)
1 pc 1/4" plywood 3 7/16" x 5 5/16"—E ⎦
2 furniture nails—headlights
2—2 1/2" no. 10 round head screws—rear axles
2—2" no. 10 round head screws—front axles
2—1 1/4" no. 6 flat head screws
2—1 1/2" no. 6 flat head screws
No. 4 finishing nails
No. 6 finishing nails
6—2" wheels

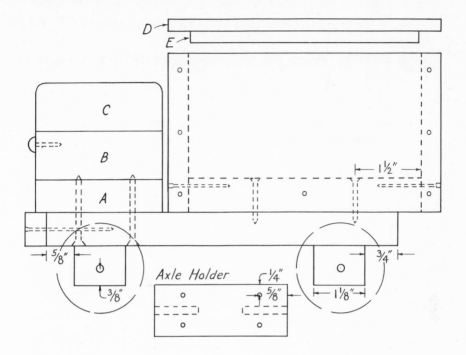

Axle Holder

Construction:

1. Glue and nail B to C and then A to B.

2. Sand the cab rounding off the top front and back edges of the C piece.

3. Drive in the headlights.

4. In the underside of the frame drill and countersink two holes for 1 1/2" screws 3/4" and 2" from the front end and centered. Glue and screw the cab to the frame letting it extend over the front about 1/4".

5. Drill pilot holes for no. 6 nails 1 1/4" in from the ends of the bumper and centered. Round off the front ends of the bumper and glue and nail it to the front end of the frame.

6. In the ends of each axle holder drill a pilot hole for the axles 3/8" from the lower edge and centered. In the 1 1/8" wide surface, locate the four pilot holes for the no. 4 nails 5/8" from the ends and 1/4" from the side edges.

7. Glue and nail the axle holders to the underside of the frame with the front holder 5/8" from the end and the rear one 3/4" from the end.

8. In the upper side of the bottom of the box drill and countersink holes 1 1/2" from either end and centered for the 1 1/4" screws.

9. In each corner of the side pieces, drill a pilot hole for the no. 4 nails 1/4" from the front and back edges and 3/8" from the top and bottom edges. Also drill a hole midway between these holes at the front, back and bottom edges.

10. In the end pieces drill pilot holes for nails 3/4" from the side edges and 1/2" from the lower edge.

11. Glue and nail the ends to the bottom and the sides to the ends and bottom.

12. Make the roof by gluing the E piece to the underside of the D piece equidistant from the end and side edges of D.

13. Apply the finish to the box, roof, frame and cab.

14. Glue and screw the box to the frame about 1/8" back from the cab.

15. Mount the wheels.

A SMALL VAN TRAILER TRUCK

Materials: Tractor

1 pc 3/4" x 3" x 7"—frame
1 pc 3/4" x 3" x 2 3/4"—A
1 pc 1 1/8" x 3" x 2 3/4"—B } cab
1 pc 1 1/8" x 3" x 2 3/4"—C
2 pc 7/8" x 1 1/8" x 3"—axle holders
1 pc 1/2" x 3/4" x 4"—bumper
2 furniture nails—headlights
2—2" no. 10 round head screws—front axles
2—2 1/2" no. 10 round head screws—rear axles
No. 4 finishing nails
No. 6 finishing nails
2—1 1/2" no. 6 flat head screws
6—2" wheels

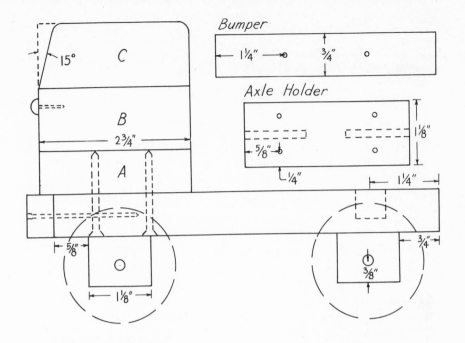

Construction: Tractor

1. Saw one end (front) of the C piece at a 15 degree angle or, make the cab without the slanted front.

2. Glue and nail B to C and then A to B.

3. Sand the assembled cab, rounding off the top front and back edges of the C piece.

4. Drive in the headlights.

5. In one end (back) of the upper side of the frame drill a 9/16″ hole, 1 1/4″ from the back edge and about 1/2″ deep equidistant from the side edges for the dowel hitch. In the underside of the frame drill and countersink two holes for screws 3/4″ and 1 3/4″ from the front end and centered.

6. Glue and screw the cab to the frame allowing it to extend about 1/4″ over the front end.

7. Drill holes for no. 6 nails 1 1/4″ from the ends of the bumper and centered. Round off the ends of the bumper and glue and nail it to the front end of the frame.

8. In the end of each axle holder drill a pilot hole for the axles 3/8″ from the lower edge and centered. In the 1 1/8″ wide surface the nail holes are 5/8″ from the ends and 1/4″ from the side edges.

9. Glue and nail the axle holders to the underside of the frame with the front one 5/8″ from the end and the rear holder 3/4″ from the end.

10. Apply the finish before mounting the wheels.

Materials: Trailer

1 pc 3/4" x 2 1/2" x 9"—bottom
2 pc 3/4" x 3 1/2" x 2 1/2"—end pieces
2 pc 7/16" x 3 1/2" x 10 1/2"—side pieces
1 pc 7/16" x 3 3/8" x 10 1/2"—A ⎞
1 pc 1/4" x 2 7/16" x 8 15/16"—B ⎬ top
1 pc 3/4" x 2 1/2" x 3 1/2"—axle holder support
1 pc 7/8" x 1 1/8" x 3"—axle holder
2—2 1/2" no. 10 round head screws—axles
2—1 1/4" no. 6 flat head screws
4—2" wheels
1 pc 1/2" dowel 1" long—hitch
No. 6 finishing nails
No. 4 finishing nails

Construction: Trailer

1. Drill pilot holes for the no. 6 nails in the bottom corners of the end pieces 1/2" up from lower edges and 1/2" in from the side edges.
2. In each side piece drill three pilot holes for no. 4 nails 3/8" in from the ends and evenly spaced. Also drill two holes along the bottom edge 3/8" from the edge and 3" from either end.
3. Drill a 1/2" hole for the hitch about 1/2" in depth and centered on the underside of the bottom 3/4" from one end (front).
4. Glue and nail the ends to the bottom and the sides to the ends and bottom.
5. In each axle holder support drill and countersink two holes for no. 6 screws 1/2" from the front and rear edges and centered. Saw off the lower edges of the support at a 30 degree angle. See diagram.
6. Make the axle holder the same as for the tractor. Glue and nail it to the support midway between the front and rear edges.
7. Glue and screw the axle holder assembly to the underside of the box 3/4" from the back end of the box and centered.
8. Make the top by gluing the B piece to the underside of the A piece 3/4" from one end of A and equidistant from the side edges.
9. Glue the dowel hitch in the hole.
10. Apply the finish before mounting the wheels.
Note: The tractor for the open trailer and the flatbed is made the same as for the van. See page 64.

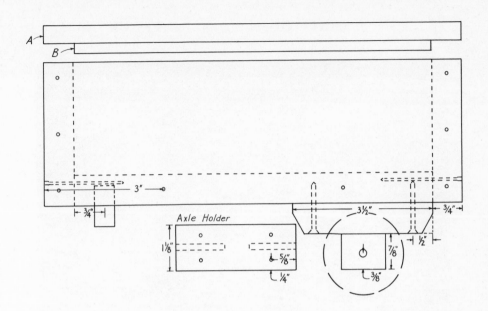

A

B

3"

¾"

Axle Holder

1⅛"

5/8"

¼"

3½"

¾"

½"

7/8"

3/8"

Materials: Small Open Trailer

1 pc 3/4" x 2 1/2" x 9"—bottom
2 pc 3/4" x 2 1/4" x 2 1/2"—ends
2 pc 7/16" x 2 1/4" x 10 1/2"—sides
1 pc 3/4" x 2 1/2" x 3 1/2"—axle holder support
1 pc 7/8" x 1 1/8" x 3"—axle holder
2—2 1/2" no. 10 round head screws—axles
2—1 1/4" no. 6 flat head screws
4—2" wheels
1 pc 1/2" dowel 1" long—hitch
No. 4 finishing nails
No. 6 finishing nails

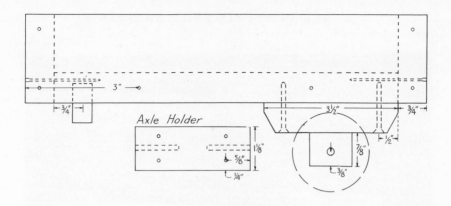

Construction: **Small Open Trailer**

1. Drill pilot holes for the no. 6 nails in the bottom corners of the end pieces 1/2″ up from lower edge and 1/2″ in from side edges.

2. In each side piece drill three pilot holes for no. 4 nails, 3/8″ in from the ends and evenly spaced. Also drill two holes along the bottom edge 3/8″ from the edge and 3″ from either end.

3. Drill a 1/2″ hole for the hitch about 1/2″ in depth and centered on the underside of the bottom 3/4″ from one end (front).

4. Glue and nail the ends to the bottom and the sides to the ends and bottom.

5. In each axle holder support, drill and countersink two holes for no. 6 screws 1/2″ from the front and rear edges and centered. Saw off the lower edges of the support at a 30 degree angle. See diagram.

6. Make the axle holder the same as for the tractor. Glue and nail it to the support midway between the front and rear edges.

7. Glue and screw the axle holder assembly to the underside of the box 3/4″ from the back end of the box and centered.

8. Glue the dowel hitch in the hole.

9. Apply the finish before mounting the wheels.

Materials: Small Flatbed Trailer

1 pc 3/4″ x 3 1/2″ x 12″—body
1 pc 3/4″ x 1 1/2″ x 3 1/2″—front end
1 pc 1/2″ x 3/4″ x 3 1/2″—A
1 pc 3/4″ x 2 1/2″ x 3 1/2″—axle holder support
1 pc 7/8″ x 1 1/8″ x 3″—axle holder
2—2 1/2″ no. 10 round head screws—axles
2—1 1/4″ no. 6 flat head screws
2—1 1/2″ no. 6 flat head screws
1 pc 1/2″ dowel 1″ long—hitch
4—2″ wheels
No. 6 finishing nails
No. 4 finishing nails

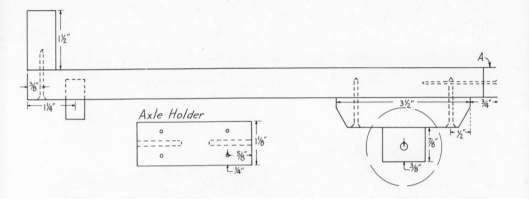

Construction: **Small Flatbed Trailer**

1. Drill a 1/2″ hole about 1/2″ in depth and 1 1/4″ from the front end of the body piece for the dowel hitch.

2. At the same end and on the same surface drill and countersink two holes for 1 1/2″ screws 3/8″ from the end and 1″ from the side edges.

3. Glue and screw the front end piece to the top surface of the body and even with the front end.

4. Drill pilot holes for no. 6 nails 3/4″ from each end of A and midway between the side edges. Glue and nail piece A to the back. end of the truck body.

5. Construct the axle holder assembly as for the small open trailer, page 69. Glue and screw this assembly to the underside of the body 3/4″ from the back end of the body and centered.

6. Apply the finish before mounting the wheels.

Section 3

A Large Open Trailer Truck
A Large Van Trailer Truck
A Large Flatbed Trailer Truck
A Dump Truck
A Tow Truck

Materials: Tractor

1 pc 1 1/8″ x 3 1/2″ x 8 1/2″—frame
1 pc 3/4″ x 3 3/8″ x 3″—A ⎫
1 pc 1 1/8″ x 3 3/8″ x 3″—B ⎬ cab
1 pc 1 1/8″ x 3 3/8″ x 3″—C ⎭
1 pc 1/2″ x 3/4″ x 4 3/4″—bumper (hardwood)
2 pc 1 1/8″ x 1 1/8″ x 3 1/2″—axle holders
2 furniture nails—headlights
1 pc 1/4″ rod 5″ long—front axle
1 pc 1/4″ rod 6″ long—rear axle
4—1/4″ Palnuts
6—2 1/4″ or 2 3/8″ wheels
2—2″ no. 6 flat head screws
No. 6 finishing naïls

Construction: Tractor

1. Saw the front end of the C piece at a 15 degree slant or, make it without the slanted front if you wish.

2. Glue and nail B to C and then A to B.

3. Sand the cab rounding off the front and rear corners of the top or C piece.

4. Drive the headlights into the front end of the B piece 3/8" in from the side and upper edges of the piece.

5. In the upper surface of the frame drill a 9/16" hole 3/4" or so deep, 1 1/4" from the back end of the frame and equidistant from the side edges. In the underside of the frame drill and countersink holes for screws 3/4" and 2 1/4" from the front end and centered.

6. Glue and screw the cab to the front end of the frame allowing it to extend about 1/4" beyond the end.

7. Drill pilot holes for nails 1 1/2" from the ends of the bumper. Round off the front ends and glue and nail the bumper to the front end of the frame using the no. 6 nails.

8. Drill 17/64" holes through the axle holders 1/2" from one side (lower) and centered. Drill four holes in each axle holder 5/8" from the ends and 1/4" from the side edges for no. 6 nails.

9. Glue and nail the axle holders to the underside of the frame with the front one 7/8" from the end and the back one 1" from the end.

10. Apply the finish and then mount the wheels.

Materials: Large Open Trailer

1 pc 3/4" x 3 1/2" x 11 1/2"—bottom
2 pc 3/4" x 2 1/2" x 3 1/2"—end pieces
2 pc 3/4" x 2 1/2" x 13"—sides
1 pc 3/4" x 3 1/2" x 5"—axle holder support
2 pc 1 1/8" x 1 1/2" x 3 1/2"—axle holders
2 pc 1/4" rod 6" long—axles
4—1/4" Palnuts
8—2 1/4" or 2 3/8" wheels
2—1 1/4" no. 6 flat head screws
4—1 1/2" no. 6 flat head screws
1 pc—1/2" dowel 1" long—hitch
No. 6 finishing nails

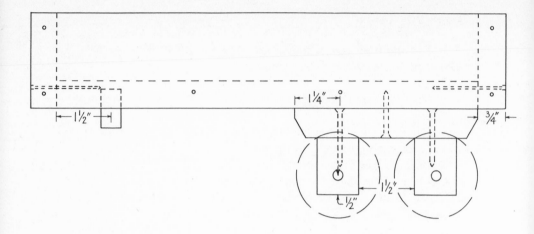

Construction: **Large Open Trailer**

1. In the two end pieces drill pilot holes for nails 1/2" from one side (lower) and 3/4" from either end.

2. In each corner of the side pieces drill a similar hole 3/8" from the edges and one midway between the two corner holes. Also, drill pilot holes along the lower edge of each side 3/8" from the lower edge and 4" from either end.

3. Drill a 1/2" hole about 1/2" deep in the underside of the bottom 1 1/2" from one end (front) and centered for the dowel hitch.

4. Drill 17/64" holes through the axle holders 1/2" from one side (lower) and centered.

5. In the axle holder support drill and countersink two holes for 1 1/4" screws 3/4" from the side edges and equidistant from the front and back edges. Saw off the lower front and back edges at a 30 degree angle.

6. Glue the axle holders to the support spaced 1 1/2" apart and equidistant from the ends of the support.

7. Drill and countersink two pilot holes for screws through the axle holder support into the axle holder. Locate these holes 1 1/4" from the ends of the support and 3/4" in from the side edges. Drive the 1 1/2" screws through the support into the axle holders.

8. Glue the axle holder assembly to the underside of the box 3/4" from the back end of the box, and centered. Drive in the screws.

9. Glue the hitch in the hole.

10. Apply the finish and mount the wheels.

Materials: Large Van Trailer

1 pc 3/4" x 4 1/8" x 11 1/2"—bottom
2 pc 3/4" x 4 1/2" x 4 1/8"—ends
2 pc 7/16" x 4 1/2" x 13"—sides
1 pc 7/16" x 5" x 13"
1 pc 1/4" x 4" x 11 3/8"—A } roof
1 pc 3/4" x 3 1/2" x 5"—axle holder support
2 pc 1 1/8" x 1 1/2" x 3 1/2"—axle holders
4—1/4" Palnuts
8—2 1/4" or 2 3/8" wheels
2—1 1/4" no. 6 flat head screws
4—1 1/2" no. 6 flat head screws
1 pc 1/2" dowel 1" long—hitch
No. 6 finishing nails
No. 4 finishing nails

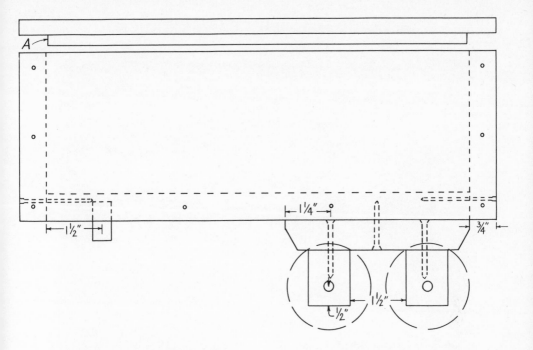

Construction: Large Van Trailer

The steps in the construction of this trailer are the same as for the large open trailer except for the roof. See page 76.

Make the roof, which will be removable, by gluing piece A to the underside of the roof piece and equidistant from the end and side edges of the roof.

A LARGE FLATBED TRAILER TRUCK

Materials: **Large Flatbed Trailer**

1 pc 3/4" x 5" x 16"—body
1 pc 1 1/8" x 1 3/4" x 5"—front end piece
1 pc 1/2" x 3/4" x 5"—back end piece
1 pc 3/4" x 3 1/2" x 5"—axle holder support
2 pc 1 1/8" x 1 1/2" x 3 1/2"—axle holders
2 pc 1/4" rod 6" long—axles
4—1/4" Palnuts
8—2 1/4" or 2 3/8" wheels
2—1 1/4" no. 6 flat head screws
7—1 1/2" no. 6 flat head screws
No. 6 finishing nails
1 pc 1/2" dowel 1" long—hitch

Construction: **Large Flatbed Trailer**

1. In the underside of the body piece drill and countersink three holes for screws 1/2" from one end (front). Locate the two outside holes 3/4" in from the side edges with one hole midway between them.

2. In the same side of the body drill a 1/2" hole about 1/2" deep 2 1/4" from the same end and centered for the hitch.

3. Glue the front end piece to the upper side of the body even with the front end. Drive 1 1/2" screws up through the body into the end piece. Glue and nail on the back end piece.

4. Construct the axle holder assembly as for the large open trailer and glue and screw it to the body 3/4" from the rear end.

5. Apply the finish before mounting the wheels.

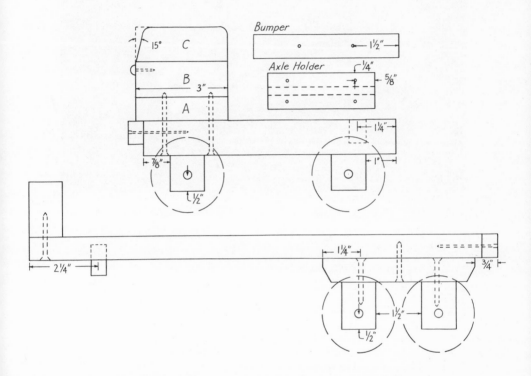

A DUMP TRUCK

Materials:

1 pc 1 1/8″ x 3 1/2″ x 9 1/2″—frame
1 pc 3/4″ x 3 3/8″ x 3 1/2″—A
1 pc 1 1/8″ x 3 3/8″ x 3 1/2″—B } cab
1 pc 1 1/8″ x 3 3/8″ x 2 1/4″—C
1 pc 1/2″ x 3/4″ x 4 3/4″—bumper (hardwood)
2—2″ no. 6 flat head screws
2 pc 1 1/8″ x 1 1/8″ x 3 1/2″ axle holders
2 furniture nails—headlights
1 pc 1/4″ rod 5″ long—front axle
1 pc 1/4″ rod 6″ long—rear axle
4—1/4″ Palnuts
6—2 1/4″ or 2 3/8″ wheels

1 pc 3/4" x 4 1/2" x 6 1/4"—bottom
2 pc 3/4" x 2 1/2" x 7 7/8"—sides
1 pc 3/4" x 2 1/2" x 4 1/2"—front end
1 pc 3/4" x 3" x 4 7/16"—tailgate
1 pc 1/2" dowel 1" long—handle
2—1 1/2" no. 8 round head screws (or pan head)
2—3/16" flat head stove bolts 1" long
1—2" butt hinge
2—1 1/2" no. 6 flat head screws
No. 6 finishing nails
No. 8 finishing nails

} box

Construction:

1. To make the cab and engine assembly glue the A piece to the B piece rounding off the front edge of the B piece.

2. Shape the top section C of the cab by cutting the front end at a 15 degree slant and then rounding off the front and rear edges. Sand the front surface of the C piece.

3. Glue the C piece to B even with the back edge and sand the assembled cab. Drive two no. 8 finishing nails up through A and B into the top piece.

4. Drive the headlights into the front end of the B piece about 3/8" from the side and top edges. Shallow holes slightly larger than the heads of the nails may be drilled for the heads.

5. In the underside of the frame drill and countersink holes for screws 3/4" and 2 1/4" from the front end and centered.

6. Glue the cab assembly to the front end of the frame allowing it to extend about 1/4" beyond the end. Drive two 2" screws through the frame into the cab and engine assembly.

7. Drill holes for nails 1 1/2" from each end of the bumper. Round off the front ends of the bumper and glue and nail it to the front end of the frame.

8. Drill holes for nails 5/8" from the ends and 1/4" from the side edges of the axle holders. Also drill 17/64" holes for the axles through the axle holders 1/2" up from the lower side and centered. Glue and nail the holders to the underside of the frame 7/8" from the front end and 1" from the back end.

9. In the bottom of the box drill and countersink two 3/16" holes 1/2" from the back edge and about 1 1/2" apart or so as to conform to the holes in the hinge being used. These holes should be equidistant

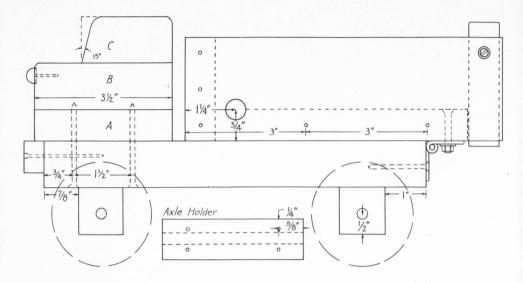

from the side edges and countersunk in the top surface of the bottom for the heads of the bolts.

10. In each side piece drill a hole for a no. 8 screw 3/8″ from the upper edge and 1/2″ from one end (back). The tailgate will swing on these screws.

11. On the outside surface of one side of the box drill a 1/2″ hole for the handle about 1/2″ deep, 3/4″ from the lower edge and 1 1/4″ from the front edge. Glue the handle in the hole.

12. At one end (front) of each side piece drill three pilot holes for nails. Locate the holes 3/8″ in from the edges with one hole midway between the other two. Also drill two more holes along the lower edge 3/8″ from the edge and 3″ and 6″ from the front end.

13. Drill pilot holes in the end of the tail gate for the no. 8 screws. Center these holes on the side edges 3/4″ down from the upper edge. Round off the upper corners of the tailgate.

14. Assemble the box by gluing and nailing the front end to the front end of the bottom piece. Be sure to have the countersunk holes for the bolts at the back and up. Glue and nail on the sides.

15. Fasten the hinge to the bottom of the box with the two bolts.

16. Varnish or paint the parts of the truck before completing the assembly.

17. Set the box on the frame with one side of the hinge against the end of the frame and equidistant from the side edges. Attach the hinge to the frame with the 1 1/2″ flat head screws.

18. Install the tailgate using the no. 8 screws.

19. Mount the wheels.

Materials:

1 pc 1 1/8″ x 3 1/2″ x 9 1/2″—frame
1 pc 3/4″ x 3 3/8″ x 3 1/2″—A ⎫
1 pc 1 1/8″ x 3 3/8″ x 3 1/2″—B ⎬ cab
1 pc 1 1/8″ x 3 3/8″ x 2 1/4″—C ⎭
1 pc 5/8″ x 1″ x 4 3/4″—bumper (hardwood)
2 pc 1 1/8″ x 1 1/8″ x 3 1/2″—axle holders
2 furniture nails—headlights
1—1/4″ rod 5″ long—front axle
1—1/4″ rod 6″ long—rear axle
4—1/4″ Palnuts
6—2 1/4″ or 2 3/8″ wheels
1 pc 3/4″ x 4 1/2″ x 6″ bottom ⎫
1 pc 3/4″ x 2 1/2″ x 4 1/2″—end ⎬ box
2 pc 3/4″ x 2 1/2″ x 7 1/2″—sides ⎭

1 pc 3/4" x 3 1/2" x 6"—D for hoist
2 pc 3/4" x 2" x 1 7/8"—E
1 pc 1/2" dowel 7 1/2" long—shaft
1 pc 1/2" dowel 1 1/4" long—handle
1 pc 1/4" dowel 1/2" long—lock
2—2" disks about 3/4" thick
1 pc sash chain (or similar) 14" long
1 S hook
1—1/2" no. 6 pan head screw
5—1 1/4" no. 6 flat head screws
4—2" no. 6 flat head screws
3 no. 10 screw eyes
20 no. 6 finishing nails
2 no. 8 finishing nails
3 washers

Construction:

1. To make the cab and engine assembly glue the A piece to the B piece rounding off the front edge of the B piece.

2. Shape the top piece C by cutting the front end at a 15 degree slant and then rounding off the front and rear edges. Sand the front surface of C.

3. Glue the cab top C to B even with the back edge and sand the assembled cab. Drive two no. 8 finishing nails through A and B into C.

4. Drive the headlights into the front end of the B piece about 3/8" from the top and side edges. Shallow holes a little larger than the heads of the furniture nails may be drilled for the heads.

5. In the underside of the frame drill and countersink holes for screws 3/4" and 2 1/4" from the front end and centered.

6. Glue the cab and engine assembly to the front end of the frame letting it extend about 1/4" beyond the end. Drive two 2" screws through the frame into the cab and engine.

7. Drill holes for nails 1 1/2" from each end of the bumper and centered. Round off the front ends of the bumper and glue and nail it to the front end of the frame.

8. Drill holes for nails 5/8" from the ends and 1/4" from the side edges of the axle holders. Also drill 17/64" holes for the axles through the axle holders 1/2" up from the lower side and centered. Glue and nail the holders to the underside of the frame 7/8" from the front end and 1" from the back end.

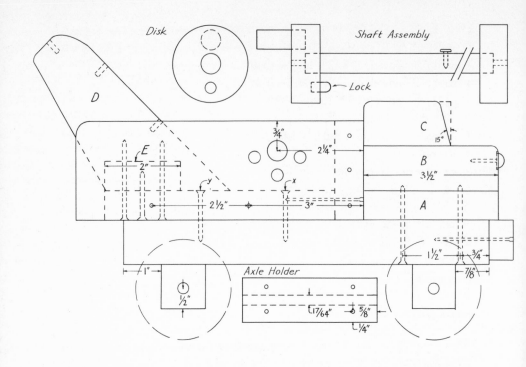

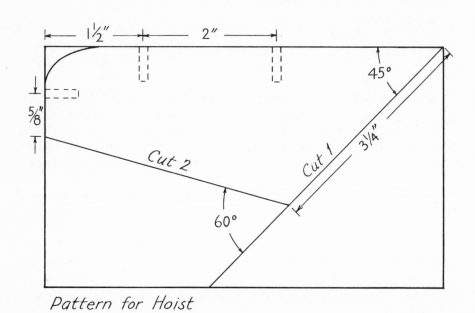

Pattern for Hoist

9. In each side of the box drill five pilot holes for nails. The holes are in 3/8" from the front and lower edges. The two holes along the lower edge are 3" and 5 1/2" from the front end of the side piece. Also drill a 17/32" hole in each side 2 1/4" from the front end and 3/4" from the upper edge. Round off the upper back corners of the sides.

10. Drill two holes for nails in the lower corners of the end piece 1/2" from the lower edge and 1" from the side edges.

11. Drill seven holes for screws in the bottom of the box as shown. Countersink holes x,y,z from the upper side and the other holes from the underside of the bottom. See diagram.

12. Nail the end piece to the front end of the bottom and the sides to the end and bottom. The sides will extend beyond the back edge of the bottom.

13. Shape the hoist and drill three pilot holes for screw eyes in the end and top edge as in the diagram.

14. Glue one of the E pieces against one side and bottom of the box even with the back end of the bottom. Glue the hoist to the bottom against the E piece. Glue the remaining E piece to the bottom between

Bottom of Box - Top View

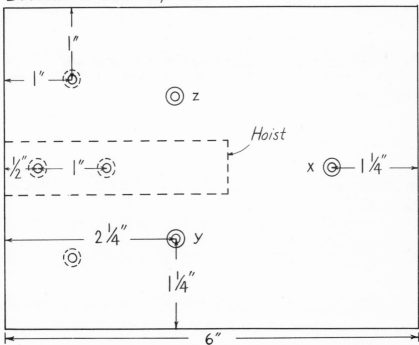

the hoist and the other side. Drive the 2″ screws up through the bottom into the hoist, and drive 1 1/4″ screws up into the E pieces.

15. Drill a pilot hole in the shaft about 3/8″ in depth for the 1/2″ screw midway between the ends of the shaft. Holes may also be drilled in the center of the ends of the shaft and disks for pan head or round head screws driven through the disks into the shaft.

16. Drill a 1/4″ hole about 1/4″ deep near the outer circumference of the inside surface of one of the disks. In this same side drill a 1/2″ hole in the center about 3/8″ in depth for the shaft to fit into. On the outside surface of this disk drill a 1/2″ hole about 3/8″ deep near the circumference for the handle. Glue the handle in the hole. Taper one end of the dowel lock and glue the other end in the 1/4″ hole. In the other disk drill a 1/2″ hole about 3/8″ deep in the center.

17. Glue the disk with the lock and handle to one end of the shaft. Insert the shaft through the holes in the sides of the box with the dowel lock against the side. Tap the disk with the hammer so that the lock makes a mark on the side of the box. Make three such marks about 3/4″ apart. Remove the shaft and drill 5/16″ holes at each mark to a depth of 3/8″ or so. The lock should fit into the holes. If it does not enlarge the holes a little.

18. Varnish or paint the parts of the truck before attaching the box to the frame.

19. Put the screw eyes into the hoist. Put a washer between the eye and the hoist.

20. Put the shaft in place again and glue on the other disk.

21. Fasten the chain to the center of the shaft with the 1/2″ pan head screw.

22. Pass the chain through the screw eyes in the hoist and attach the S hook to the end.

23. Mount the wheels.

Section 4

Materials: **Tractor**

1 pc 3/4" x 1 5/8" x 9 1/2"—A—base

2 pc 3/4" x 1 5/8" x 6"—B—engine

1 pc 1 1/8" x 2 1/2" x 4 3/8"—rear axle holder

1 pc 1 1/8" x 1 1/2" x 1 5/8"—C ⎫
1 pc 3/4" x 1 1/4" x 1 7/8"—D ⎬ front axle holder

1 pc 7/16" x 3/4" x 3/4" ⎫
1 pc 1/4" x 3/4" x 1"—back ⎬ seat

1 pc 1/4" rod 7 1/2" long—rear axle

1 pc 1/4" rod 3 3/8" long—front axle

5—1 1/4" no. 6 flat head screws

4—1/4" Palnuts

2—2" no. 6 flat head screws

1—1 1/2" no. 8 round head screw—shaft ⎫
1—1" wheel ⎬ steering wheel assembly
2—3/16" ferrules or piece of tubing—spacer ⎭

2—4" wheels 1 1/8" thick—rear

2—2" wheels 1/2" thick—front

No. 4 finishing nails

3 furniture nails

1 no. 10 ceiling hook

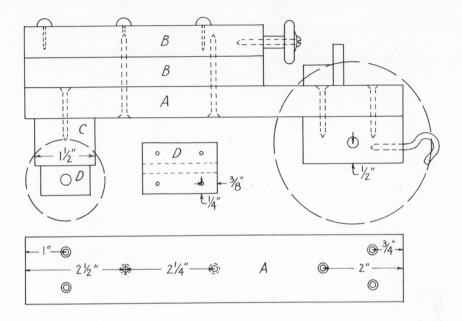

Construction: Tractor

1. Prepare the base first by drilling two holes for screws in one side (upper) of piece A 3/4" from one end (back), and two holes 1" from the other end. Locate these four holes 3/8" from the side edges. Also drill a screw hole 1 3/4" from the back end and centered. Countersink these holes. Drill two more holes 2 1/2" and 4 3/4" from the front. Countersink these holes on the underside of A.

2. Glue piece C to the underside of the base 1/4" from the front end. Drive two 1 1/4" screws through the base into C. Drill a 17/64" hole lengthwise through the center of piece D for the front axle. Also drill four pilot holes for nails 3/8" from the ends of D and 1/4" in from the front and back edges. Center D on C and glue and nail in place. D will extend 1/8" beyond C at each end.

3. To make the engine, glue the two B pieces together. Drill a pilot hole for the steering wheel shaft in one end of the engine 1/2" down from the upper surface and centered.

4. In the back surface of the rear axle holder, drill a pilot hole for the screw hook midway between the ends and 3/8" from the lower edge. Drill a 17/64" hole lengthwise through the holder 1/2" from the lower edge and centered.

5. Attach the axle holder to the base even with the back end with glue and three 1 1/4" screws through A into the holder.

6. Drive one furniture nail into the engine 1/2" from the front end and another one 1 1/2" from the back end and centered. Drive

the other nail in 2 1/2" from the front end and 3/8" from one side edge. A piece of 1/4" dowel 1" long may be used to represent the muffler instead of this last nail. Glue the engine to the base and drive the 2" screws up through the base into the engine.

7. Install the steering wheel.

8. Glue the seat in place about 1" back from the end of the engine.

9. Screw in the hitch.

10. Apply the finish and then mount the wheels.

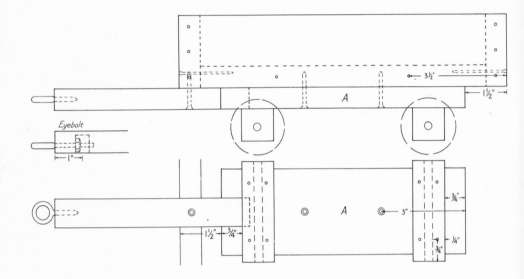

Materials: **Wagon**

1 pc 3/4" x 4 1/2" x 10 1/4"—bottom ⎫
2 pc 3/4" x 2 1/2" x 4 1/2"—ends ⎬ box
2 pc 3/4" x 2 1/2" x 11 3/4"—sides ⎭
1 pc 3/4" x 3" x 8 3/4"—A—axle holder support
1 pc 3/4" x 1" x 7"—B—tongue
2 pc 1 1/8" x 1 1/8" x 3 1/2"—axle holders
4—2" wheels
3—1 1/4" no. 6 flat head screws
2—1/4" rods about 5" long—axles
4—1/4" Palnuts
1—no. 10 screw eye *or* a 3/16" eye bolt 2" long
No. 6 finishing nails

1. In each end piece, drill two pilot holes for nails 1" from either side edge and 1/2" from the lower edge.

2. In the side pieces, drill holes for nails 3/8" in from the ends and side edges. There are three holes at each end and two along the lower edges 3 1/2" from the ends of the side pieces.

3. Glue and nail the ends to the bottom and the sides to the ends and bottom.

4. In the center of one end of A cut an opening 1" wide and about 1" long for the end of the tongue to fit into. In the underside of this same piece drill and countersink two holes for screws 3" from each end and centered.

5. In each axle holder drill 4 holes for nails 3/4" from the ends and 1/4" from the side edges. Drill a 17/64" hole lengthwise through the axle holders 1/2" from the lower edge and centered. Glue and nail the axle holders to the holder support A 3/4" from each end. They will extend a 1/4" at each end.

6. Glue and screw piece A to the underside of the box 1 1/2" from each end and centered.

7. Insert the screw eye into the center of one end of the tongue. Or, an eye bolt may be used instead by drilling a 3/16" hole into the end of the tongue to a depth of 1" or so and 1/4" from the lower side. Then drill a 1/2" hole about 5/8" deep 1" back from the end in the lower side of the tongue. Insert the eye bolt into the 3/16" hole and screw it into the nut placed in the 1/2" hole.

8. Insert the end of the tongue into the opening cut for it and glue fast. Drill and countersink a pilot hole for a screw through the tongue into the front end of the box.

9. Apply the finish before mounting the wheels.

A BULLDOZER

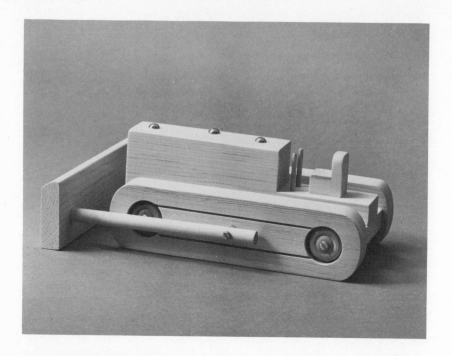

Materials: Bulldozer

1 pc 3/4" x 1 3/4" x 9 1/2"—A
2 pc 3/4" x 1 3/4" x 6"—B—engine
1 pc 3/4" x 3 1/2" x 9"—C
1 pc 3/4" x 2 1/2" x 9"—blade
2 pc 1/2" dowel 7 1/4" long—blade arms
2 pc 1 1/8" x 2 1/2" x 9 1/2"—tracks
1 pc 3/4" x 1" x 3/4"
1 pc 7/16" x 1" x 1 1/2" } seat
4—2" no. 8 pan head screws
2—1 1/4" no. 8 pan head screws
2—2" no. 6 flat head screws
2—1 1/4" no. 6 flat head screws
3 furniture nails
4—1 1/4" wheels or disks
2 pc 3/16" dowel 1 3/4" long—control levers
2 washers

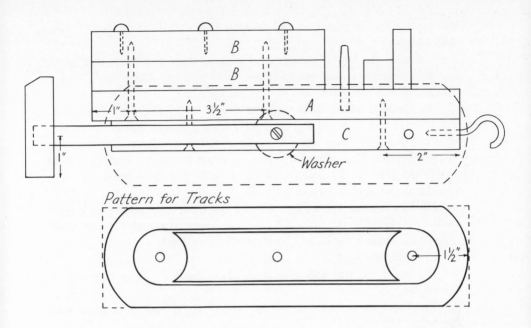

Pattern for Tracks

Construction: Bulldozer

1. Glue the two B pieces together to make the engine. Sand piece A and glue the engine to one end. Sand this completed assembly.

2. In the underside of piece A drill and countersink holes for 2″ flat head screws 1″ and 4 1/2″ back from the front end and centered. In the upper side of A drill two 3/16″ holes about 1/2″ in depth 1/2″ back from the engine and 1/2″ in from either side edge for the control levers.

3. Drive the 2″ flat head screws through A into the engine.

4. In piece C drill and countersink holes for the 1 1/4″ flat head screws 2″ from each end and centered.

5. With a Greenlee or Forstner type bit drill 1 3/8″ holes 1 1/2″ from each end of the tracks and centered. Make the holes just deep enough so that the head of the screw when put through the wheel or disk will be about flush with the outer surface of the track. Also drill a pilot hole for a no. 8 screw in each track midway between the ends and centered.

6. Connect the 1 3/8″ holes with saw cuts about 1/8″ in depth and 9/16″ from the side edges. Round off the ends of the track as shown.

7. Glue piece C to the inside of the tracks midway between the top and bottom edges and 1/4″ from either end.

8. Drill pilot holes for screws through the center of the 1 3/8″ holes

into piece C. Set a wheel or disk in each hole and drive in the 2″ pan head screws.

9. Center the engine assembly on piece C even with back end of C and glue in place. It will extend about 1/2″ in front. Drive the 1 1/4″ flat head screws through C into the engine assembly.

10. Drive furniture nails into the engine 3/4″ from the front end and 1″ from the back end and centered. Locate the other nail 3″ from the front end and 1/2″ from one side edge.

11. In each blade arm drill holes for no. 8 screws 1″ from one end. Attach the arms to the tracks with the 1 1/4″ pan head screws putting a washer between the arm and the track.

12. Saw off the upper front edge of the blade at a 30 degree angle. Drill 1/2″ holes in the blade 1″ from the lower edge and 1 1/4″ from either end. These holes should be about 1/2″ in depth.

13. Glue the blade to the arms.

14. Make the seat and glue it in place about 1″ from the end of the engine.

15. Taper the upper ends of the control levers and drive them into the holes.

A FLATBED TRUCK FOR THE BULLDOZER

Materials: Tractor

1 pc 1 1/8″ x 3 1/2″ x 8 1/2″—frame
1 pc 3/4″ x 3 3/8″ x 3″—A ⎫
1 pc 1 1/8″ x 3 3/8″ x 3″—B ⎬ cab
1 pc 1 1/8″ x 3 3/8″ x 3″—C ⎭
1 pc 1/2″ x 3/4″ x 4 3/4″—bumper (hardwood)
2 pc 1 1/8″ x 1 1/8″ x 3 1/2″—axle holders
2 furniture nails—headlights
1 pc 1/4″ rod 5″ long—front axle
1 pc 1/4″ rod 6″ long—rear axle
4—1/4″ Palnuts
6—2 1/4″ or 2 3/8″ wheels
2—2″ no. 6 flat head screws
No. 6 finishing nails

Axle Holder for Trailer

Axle Holder

Construction: Tractor

1. Saw the front end of the C piece at a 15 degree slant or, make it without the slanted front if you wish.

2. Glue and nail B to C and then A to B.

3. Sand the cab rounding off the front and rear corners of the top or C piece.

4. Drive the headlights into the front end of the B piece 3/8" in from the side and upper edges of the piece.

5. In the upper surface of the frame drill a 9/16" hole 3/4" or so deep, 1 1/4" from the back end of the frame and equidistant from the side edges. In the underside of the frame drill and countersink holes for screws 3/4" and 2 1/4" from the front end and centered.

6. Glue and screw the cab to the front end of the frame allowing it to extend about 1/4" beyond the end.

7. Drill pilot holes for nails 1 1/2" from the ends of the bumper. Round off the front ends and nail and glue the bumper to the front end of the frame.

8. Drill 17/64" holes through the axle holders 1/2" from one side (lower) and centered. Drill four holes in each axle holder 5/8" from the ends and 1/4" from the side edges for no. 6 nails.

9. Glue and nail the axle holders to the underside of the frame with the front one 7/8" from the end and the back one 1" from the end.

10. Apply the finish and then mount the wheels.

Materials: Trailer

1 pc 3/4" x 7" x 12"—A
1 pc 3/4" x 7" x 6"—B
1 pc 1 1/8" x 1" x 7"—C
1 pc 1/2" x 3/4" x 7"—D
2 pc 3/4" x 1 1/2" x 7"—axle holders
1 pc 1/2" dowel 1" long—hitch
2 pc 1/4" rod 9 1/2" long—axles
4—1/4" Palnuts
8—2" wheels
8—1 1/4" no. 6 flat head screws
2—1 1/2" no. 6 flat head screws
3—2" no. 6 pan head screws
No. 6 finishing nails

Construction: Trailer

1. Drill and countersink two holes 1/2" from one end (front) and 1 1/4" in from the side edges of piece A.
2. In piece D drill holes for nails 3/4" from either end and centered. Glue and nail D to the back end of A.
3. Glue the C piece, with the 1 1/8" surface down, to the front end of the A piece. Drive the two 1 1/2" screws up through A into C.
4. In the B piece drill a 1/2" hole about 1/2" in depth 1" from one end (front) and centered for the hitch. Round off the front corners of B.
5. In the other end of B or back, drill three holes for screws located 3/4" from the side edges and 1/2" from the end with one hole in the center.
6. Glue the dowel hitch in the hole drilled in the underside of the B piece. Then glue B to C and drive in the pan head screws.
7. In one 1 1/2" side of each axle holder saw a groove lengthwise in the center slightly over 1/4" x 1/4" or so that the axle will turn freely in the groove. In the opposite side drill and countersink holes for screws 1" from the ends and 5/16" from the side edges.
8. Glue and screw the axle holders to the underside of the A piece. Locate the rear holder 1" from the end of A and space them 1" apart.
9. Apply the finish before mounting the wheels.

A CRANE AND TRAILER TRUCK

Materials: **Crane**

1 pc 3/4" x 2 1/2" x 9"—A
2 pc 3/4" x 1" x 5 1/2"—B
1 pc 3/4" x 2 1/2" x 14"—boom
2 pc 3/4" x 3 3/4" x 5"—sides
1 pc 3/4" x 4" x 6"—roof
3—2" wooden disks 3/4" thick
10—1 1/4" no. 6 pan head screws (or round head)
1—1/2" no. 6 pan head screw (or round head)
1—2" no. 8 pan head screw (or round head)
2—2" no. 6 flat head screws
4—screw eyes
2' chain (sash chain or lighter)
1 small S hook
1 pc 1/2" dowel 5 1/2" long—shaft
1 pc 1/4" dowel 1/2" long—lock

1 pc 1/2" dowel 1 1/4" long—handle
1 pc 1/2" dowel 1 1/2" long—control lever
No. 4 finishing nails
5 washers

(The screw eyes should be large enough so that the chain will slide easily through the eye. A brass chain obtainable at a hardware store is very good, or use window sash chain).

Construction: **Crane**

1. Shape the boom as shown or use a piece 3/4" x 1 1/2" x 14" and do not taper. In either case, saw one end (lower) at a 45 degree angle. Drill a pilot hole for a screw eye in the center of the upper end and also at 2 1/2", 6 3/4" and 11" from the same end and centered on the upper edge of the boom. Round off the upper corner of the boom.

2. In one side (upper) of the A piece drill a 1/2" hole for the control lever about 1/2" in depth 1 1/2" from one end (back) and centered. Round off the corners of this end. Turn the piece over. Drill and countersink two holes for the 2" screws 3/4" and 1 3/4" from the front end of A and centered. If the boom is made from material 1 1/2" wide, locate these two holes 1/2" and 1" from the front end of A. Drill a hole for the no. 8 screw through the center of the A piece. Insert the control lever.

3. Through each side piece drill a hole slightly larger than 1/2", located 1" from the upper edge and 3" from the front end. Also in each side drill two holes for screws 3/8" from the lower edge and 3/4" in from the side edges.

4. In one of the 3/4" sides of each B piece, drill pilot holes for nails 1 1/2" from either end and centered. Round off the upper front and back corners.

5. Glue one B piece to each side of the boom even with the lower end and front of the boom.

6. Glue and nail the boom assembly to piece A even with the front end of A and centered.

7. Drive the 2" flat head screws up through A into the boom.

8. Glue and screw the sides to the A piece with the front edge of each side 1" from the front end of A.

9. Drill a pilot hole in the shaft about 3/8" deep and midway between the ends for the 1/2" screw. Holes may also be drilled in the center of the ends of the shaft and disks for pan head or round head screws driven through the disks into the shaft.

10. Drill a 1/4" hole about 1/4" in depth near the outer circumference of the inside surface of one of the disks. In this same side drill

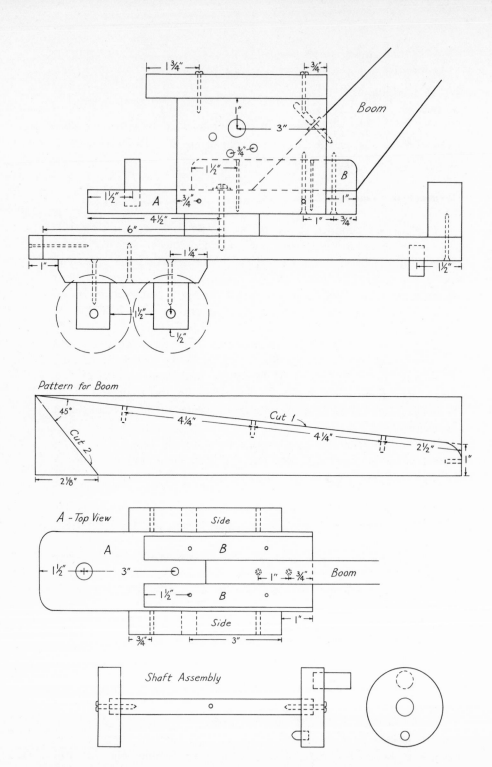

Boom

3″

B

A

1½″

¾″

4½″

6″

1″

1″

¾″

1″

1¼″

1½″

1½″

½″

Pattern for Boom

45°

Cut 2

Cut 1

4¼″

4¼″

2½″

1″

2⅛″

A - Top View

Side

A

B

B

Boom

1½″

3″

1½″

1″

¾″

3″

Side

1″

¾″

3″

Shaft Assembly

a 1/2" hole in the center about 3/8" in depth for the shaft to fit into. On the outside surface of the same disk drill a 1/2" hole about 3/8" deep near the circumference for the handle. Glue the handle in this hole. Taper one end of the dowel lock and glue the other end in the 1/4" hole. In the other disk drill a 1/2" hole about 3/8" deep in the center of one side.

11. Glue the disk with the lock and handle to one end of the shaft. Insert the shaft through the holes in the sides with the dowel lock against the side. Tap the disk with the hammer so that the lock makes a mark on the box. Make three such marks about 3/4" apart. Remove the shaft and drill 5/16" holes at each mark to a depth of 3/8" or so. The lock should fit into the holes. If it does not enlarge the holes.

12. Varnish or paint the parts including the roof.

13. Put the shaft in place again and glue on the other disk. Put the screw eyes into the boom, with a washer between the eye and the boom.

14. Fasten the chain to the center of the shaft with the 1/2" pan head screw.

15. Pass the chain through the screw eyes in the hoist and attach the S hook to the end.

16. Round off the two back corners of the roof. Drill two holes for screws 1 3/4" from this end and 3/8" from the side edges, and two holes 3/4" from the front end and 3/8" from the side edges. Note: Before attaching the roof make the tractor and trailer for the crane.

TRAILER TRUCK FOR THE CRANE

Materials: **Tractor**

1 pc 1 1/8" x 3 1/2" x 8 1/2"—frame
1 pc 3/4" x 3 3/8" x 3"—A ⎫
1 pc 1 1/8" x 3 3/8" x 3"—B ⎬ cab
1 pc 1 1/8" x 3 3/8" x 3"—C ⎭
1 pc 1/2" x 3/4" x 4 3/4"—bumper (hardwood)
2 pc 1 1/8" x 1 1/8" x 3 1/2"—axle holders
2 furniture nails—headlights
1 pc 1/4" rod 5" long—front axle
1 pc 1/4" rod 6" long—rear axle
4—1/4" Palnuts
6—2 1/4" or 2 3/8" wheels
2—2" no. 6 flat head screws
No. 6 finishing nails

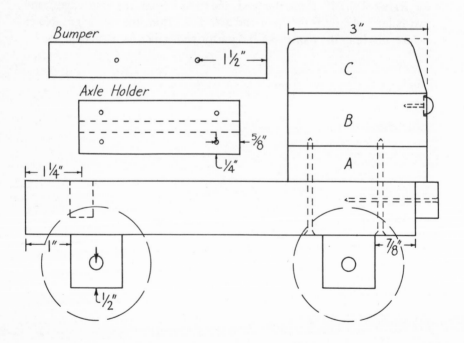

1. Saw the front end of the C piece at a 15 degree slant or, make it without the slanted front if you wish.

2. Glue and nail B to C and then A to B.

3. Sand the cab rounding off the front and rear corners of the top or C piece.

4. Drive the headlights into the front end of the B piece 3/8" in from the side and upper edges of the piece.

5. In the upper surface of the frame drill a 9/16" hole 3/4" or so deep, 1 1/4" from the back end of the frame and equidistant from the side edges. In the underside of the frame drill and countersink holes for screws 3/4" and 2 1/4" from the front end and centered.

6. Glue and screw the cab to the front end of the frame allowing it to extend about 1/4" beyond the end.

7. Drill pilot holes for nails 1 1/2" from the ends of the bumper. Round off the front ends and glue and nail the bumper to the front end of the frame.

8. Drill 17/64" holes through the axle holders 1/2" from one side (lower) and centered. Drill four holes in each axle holder 5/8" from the ends and 1/4" from the side edges for no. 6 nails.

9. Glue and nail the axle holders to the underside of the frame with the front one 7/8" from the end and the back one 1" from the end.

10. Apply the finish and then mount the wheels.

Materials: Trailer

1 pc 3/4" x 5" x 14"—body
1 pc 1 1/8" x 1 3/4" x 5"—front end
1 pc 1/2" x 3/4" x 5"—rear end
1 pc 3/4" x 3 1/2" x 5"—axle holder support
2 pc 1 1/8" x 1 1/2" x 3 1/2"—axle holders
2 pc 1/4" rod 6" long—axles
4—1/4" Palnuts
8—2 1/4" or 2 3/8" wheels
2—1 1/4" no. 6 flat head screws
7—1 1/2" no. 6 flat head screws
1 pc 1/2" dowel 1" long—hitch
No. 6 finishing nails

Construction: Trailer

1. In the underside of the body at the front end drill and countersink three holes for screws. Locate them 1/2" from the front edge with the two outside holes 3/4" from the side edges and the other hole in the center. Also in the underside drill a 1/2" hole about 1/2" in depth for the hitch. The hole should be 1 1/2" from the front end and centered. In the top surface of the body drill a pilot hole for the no. 8 screw 6" from the back end and centered.

2. Glue the end piece in place even with the front end of the body and drive in the 1 1/2" screws.

3. Glue and nail the back end piece on.

4. Drill 17/64" holes through the axle holders 1/2" from one side (lower) and centered.

5. In the axle holder support drill and countersink two holes for screws 3/4" in from the side edges and midway between the front and back edges. Saw off the lower front and back edges at a 30 degree angle.

6. Glue the axle holders to the support spaced 1 1/2" apart and equidistant from the ends of the support. Drill and countersink two pilot holes for screws through the axle holder support into each axle holder. Locate these holes 1 1/4" from the ends of the support and 3/4" in from the side edges. Drive the 1 1/2" screws through the support into the axle holders.

7. Glue the axle holder assembly to the underside of the body 1" from the back end and centered. Drive in the 1 1/4" screws.

8. Glue the hitch in the hole.

9. Apply the finish to all parts.

10. Drill a hole through the center of the disk and fasten the crane to the trailer with the disk between the crane and the trailer. Use the no. 8 pan or round head screw with a washer underneath the head of the screw.

11. Fasten the roof on with the pan or round head screws.

12. Mount the wheels.

A CRAWL CRANE

The materials for and the construction of this crane are the same as for the crane on the flatbed trailer truck. Page 106. After completing the crane, except for putting the roof on, make the track assembly as described below.

Materials: **Track Assembly**

2 pc 1 1/8" x 2 1/2" x 10"—tracks
1 pc 3/4" x 4" x 9"—C
1 pc 3/4" x 4" x 5"—D
4—1 1/4" wheels or disks
4—2" no. 8 pan or round head screws
1—2 1/2" no. 8 pan or round head screw
2—1 1/4" no. 6 flat head screws

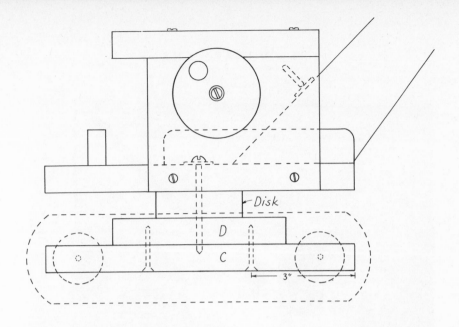

Pattern for Tracks

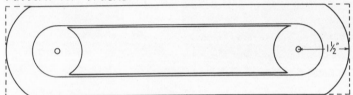

Construction: Track Assembly

1. With a Greenlee or Forstner type bit drill 1 3/8″ holes about 3/8″ in depth with centers 1 1/2″ from each end of the tracks and midway between the upper and lower edges.

2. Connect the holes with saw cuts about 1/8″ deep and 9/16″ from the side edges. Round off the ends of the tracks. See diagram.

3. Drill and countersink holes in piece C for the 1 1/4″ screws 3″ from either end and centered. Glue piece C to the inside of the tracks midway between the upper and lower edges and 1/2″ from either end.

4. Drill pilot holes for no. 8 screws through the center of the 1 3/8″ holes in the tracks into piece C. Set a wheel or disk in each hole and drive in the screws.

5. Drill a pilot hole in the center of piece D for the 2 1/2″ screw. Glue D to C equidistant from the ends of C. Drive the 1 1/4″ screws through C into D.

6. Varnish or paint the track assembly.

7. Fasten the crane to piece D with the disk between the crane and D. Use the 2 1/2″ screw with a washer underneath the head of the screw.

8. Put on the roof.

A STATIONARY CRANE

The materials for and the construction of this crane are the same as for the crane on the flatbed trailer truck. Page 106. After completing the crane, except for putting the roof on, make the base for it.

Materials: **Base**

2 pc 3/4" x 4 3/4" x 10"—X ⎫
1 pc 3/4" x 7 1/2" x 12"—Y ⎬ base
2—2" no. 6 flat head screws
1—2 1/2" no. 8 pan or round head screw

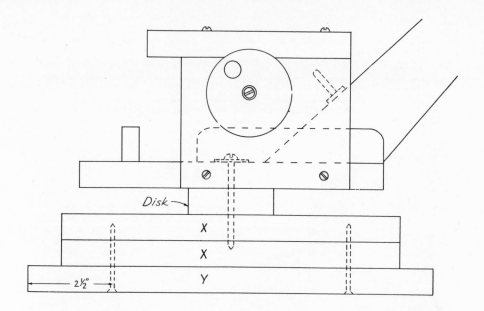

Disk

X

X

Y

2½"

Construction: **Base**

1. Round off the corners of the Y piece.

2. Glue the two X pieces together and sand the sides, ends and upper surface. In the center of the X pieces drill a pilot hole for the No. 8 screw.

3. Glue the X pieces to Y equidistant from the end and side edges of Y.

4. In the underside of the Y piece drill and countersink two holes for screws 2 1/2" from the ends and centered. Drive in the 2" screws.

Note: If the toymaker wishes to make this a mobile crane casters can be installed in the underside of the Y piece 3/4" from the end and side edges.

5. Varnish or paint the base.

6. Fasten the crane to the base with the disk between the crane and base. Use the 2 1/2" screw with a washer underneath the head of the screw. Put on the roof.

A ROLLER

Materials:

1 pc 1 3/4″ x 2 1/2″ x 5 3/4″—A—engine
1 pc 3/4″ x 1 3/4″ x 6″—B } frame
1 pc 3/4″ x 1 3/4″ x 3″—C
1 pc 3/4″ x 1″ x 3/4″
1 pc 7/16″ x 1″ x 1 1/4″—back } seat
1 cylinder 3″ in diameter by 3″ long—drum
2 wheels 1 1/8″ thick by 4″ in diameter
1 pc 1/4″ rod 5 3/8″ long—rear axle
1 pc 1/4″ rod 3 7/8″ long—front axle
4—1/4″ Palnuts
8 washers to fit 1/4″ rod
2—5/16″ ferrules—spacers
1 drum holder—can be made from aluminum stock 1/8″ x 3/4″
2—3/4″ no. 6 round head screws
1—1″ wheel
1—1 1/4″ no. 8 round head screw
1—3/16″ ferrule } steering wheel assembly
2—no. 8 machine screw washers
4—1 1/4″ no. 6 flat head screws

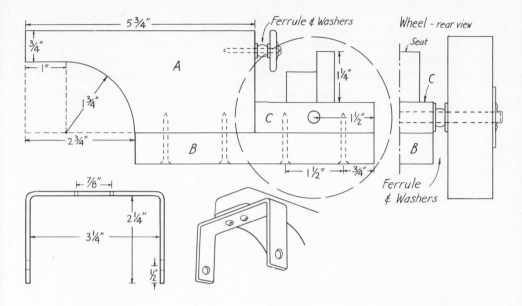

Construction:

1. Shape piece A as shown. Drill a pilot hole for the steering wheel shaft (screw) 1/2" from the upper side and centered. See diagram.

2. In piece B drill and countersink four holes 3/4" and 2 1/4" from each end and equidistant from the side edges.

3. Drill a 17/64" hole through piece C for the axle. Center the hole on the 3/4" x 3" side.

4. Glue the C piece to one end (back) of B. Drive two screws through B into C.

5. Glue piece A to B against the end of the C piece. Drive the other two 1 1/4" screws through B into A.

6. Install the steering wheel by inserting the screw through the wheel, washer, ferrule and another washer. (A short piece of metal or plastic tubing may be used on the steering wheel post for the spacer instead of the ferrule.)

7. Make the seat and glue it to C about 1" from the back end of piece A.

8. Shape the metal holder for the roller drum as shown in the diagram. Attach it to the underside of A with the 3/4" screws about 1/8" from the front end. The holder may be glued on first to locate it, and then pilot holes drilled for the screws.

Note: All parts should now be varnished or painted before completing steps 9-10.

9. Drill a 17/64" hole lengthwise through the center of the drum and set it in the holder placing a washer at each end. Insert the axle

and drive on the Palnuts. (Four 3/4″ x 3 1/2″ x 3 1/2″ pieces may be laminated and then turned on a lathe to make a drum 3″ in diameter and 3″ long.)

10. When installing the wheels put a washer on the outside of each wheel between the Palnut and the wheel. Pass the axle through the wheel putting on a washer, a ferrule and another washer between each wheel and the frame. (Fender washers to fit 1/4″ rod are very good for the outside of the wheels or at the end of the roller drum.)

A ROLLER WITH A ROOF

Materials:

1 pc 1 3/4" x 2 1/2" x 5 3/4"—A—engine

1 pc 3/4" x 1 3/4" x 6"—B
1 pc 3/4" x 1 3/4" x 3"—C } frame

1 pc 3/4" x 1" x 3/4"
1 pc 7/16" x 1" x 1 1/4"—back } seat

1 cylinder 3" in diameter by 3" long—drum

1 pc 3/4" x 2 1/2" x 4"—roof
2 pc 5/16" dowel 2" long—front posts } roof assembly
2 pc 5/16" dowel 3 3/4" long—back posts

2 wheels 1 1/8" thick by 4" in diameter

1 pc 1/4" rod 5 3/8" long—rear axle

1 pc 1/4" rod 3 7/8" long—front axle

4—1/4" Palnuts

8 washers to fit 1/4" rod

2—5/16" ferrules—spacers

1 drum holder—can be made from aluminum stock 1/8" x 3/4"

2—3/4" no. 6 round head screws
1—1" wheel
1—1 1/4" no. 8 round head screw ⎫
1—3/16" ferrule   ⎬ steering wheel assembly
2—no. 8 machine screw washers   ⎭
4—1 1/4" no. 6 flat head screws

Construction:

1. Shape piece A as shown. Drill a pilot hole for the steering wheel shaft (screw) 1/2" from the upper side and centered. See diagram.

2. In piece B drill and countersink four holes 3/4" and 2 1/4" from each end and equidistant from the side edges.

3. Drill a 17/64" hole through piece C for the axle. Center the hole on the 3/4" x 3" side.

4. Glue the C piece to one end (back) of B. Drive two screws through B into C.

5. Glue piece A to B against the end of the C piece. Drive the other two 1 1/4" screws through B into A.

6. Install the steering wheel by inserting the screw through the wheel, washer, ferrule and another washer. (A short piece of metal or plastic tubing may be used on the steering wheel post for the spacer instead of the ferrule.)

7. Make the seat and glue it to C about 1" from the back end of piece A.

8. Shape the metal holder for the roller drum as shown in the diagram. Attach it to the underside of A with the 3/4" screws about 1/8" from the front end. The holder may be glued on first to locate it, and then pilot holes drilled for the screws.

9. In the top of the C piece drill two 5/16" holes 1/2" from the back edge, 3/8" in from the side edges and 1/2" deep.

10. In piece A drill two 5/16" holes 1/2" from the back edge, 3/8" from the side edges and 1/2" in depth.

11. In the underside of the roof drill four holes 1/2" from the ends, 3/4" from the side edges and 1/2" deep.

12. Round off the top side edges of the roof.

13. Put glue in the holes in the roof and drive in the dowel posts.

Note: All parts should now be varnished or painted before completing steps 14-16.

14. Drill a 17/64" hole lengthwise through the center of the drum and set it in the holder placing a washer at each end. Insert the axle and drive on the Palnuts. (Four 3/4" x 3 1/2" x 3 1/2" pieces may be laminated and then turned on a lathe to make a drum 3" in diameter and 3" long.)

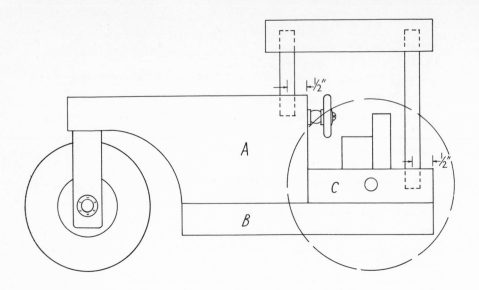

15. When installing the wheels put a washer on the outside of each wheel between the Palnut and the wheel. Pass the axle through the wheel putting on a washer, a ferrule and another washer between each wheel and the frame. (Fender washers to fit 1/4″ rod are very good for the outside of the wheels or at the end of the roller drum.)

16. Put glue in the four holes in the roller and install the roof assembly.

Section 5

A Small Train (engine, tender, freight car, gondola car, caboose)
A Freight Train (engine, tender, gondola car, box car, flat car, caboose)
A Passenger Train (Diesel engine, baggage car, passenger car)

Materials: **Engine**

1 pc 3/4" x 2" x 8"—base
2 pc 3/4" x 1 7/8" x 7"—boiler
1 pc 7/16" x 1 7/8" x 5"—boiler top
1 pc 1/2" x 1 7/8" x 2 1/2"—cab roof
1 pc 1/2" x 3/4" x 2 1/2"—A
1 pc 1/2" dowel 3/4" long—smokestack
6—2" wheels
6—1 1/2" no. 10 round head screws—axles
2—1 1/2" no. 6 flat head screws
3 furniture nails—domes and headlight

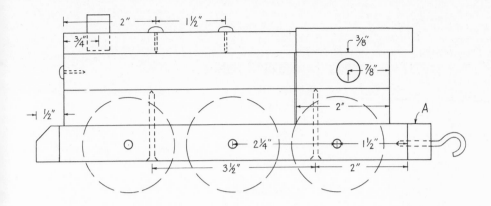

Construction: **Engine**

1. In each side edge of the base drill three pilot holes for the screw axles 2 1/4″ apart and centered. Locate the first hole 1 1/2″ from one end (rear) of the base. In the underside of the base, drill and countersink two holes 2″ and 5 1/2″ from the rear end for screws to fasten the boiler to the base.

2. Saw off both corners of the front end of the base, with the miter gauge set at a 60 degree angle, to form the cowcatcher. Then cut off the top of the front edge at a 45 degree angle.

3. In the center of one side of piece A drill a pilot hole for the screw hook. Glue the A piece to the back end of the base.

4. Glue the two pieces together to make the boiler and cab.

5. In each side of the cab drill a 1/2″ hole about 1/4″ in depth 7/8″ from the rear end and 3/8″ down from the top edge for windows. Also on each side of the boiler make a shallow vertical cut with a thin saw blade, 2″ from the rear end.

6. Glue the boiler top to the boiler even with the front end and round off the side edges. Drill a 1/2″ hole about 3/8″ deep and 3/4″ from the front end of the top for the smokestack.

7. Glue and screw the boiler and cab assembly to the base about 1/2″ back from the tip of the cowcatcher.

8. Drive the domes into the top of the boiler 2″ and 3 1/2″ from the front end and centered. Drive the headlight into the center of the front of the upper section of the boiler.

9. Glue the cab roof in place against the rear end of the top of the boiler.

10. Paint or varnish the engine.

11. Mount the wheels and screw in the coupler.

Materials for all cars:

Tender
2 pc 7/16" x 1 1/2" x 1 3/4"—ends
2 pc 7/16" x 1 1/2" x 5"—sides
1 pc 1/4" x 2 5/8" x 5"—bottom

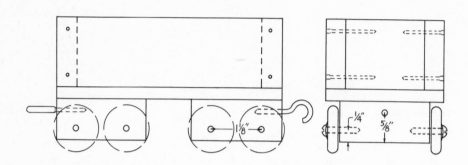

Gondola Car
2 pc 7/16" x 1" x 1 3/4"—ends
2 pc 7/16" x 1" x 7"—sides
1 pc 1/4" x 2 5/8" x 7"—bottom

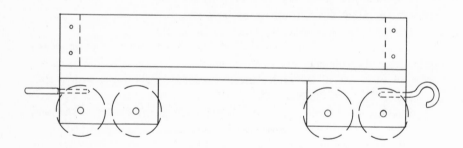

Box Car
2 pc 7/16" x 2" x 1 3/4"—ends
2 pc 7/16" x 2" x 7"—sides
1 pc 1/4" x 2 5/8" x 7"—bottom
1 pc 1/4" x 2 5/8" x 7"
1 pc 1/4" x 1 11/16" x 6 1/16"—A } roof
1 pc 1/16" x 7/16" x 7"—catwalk

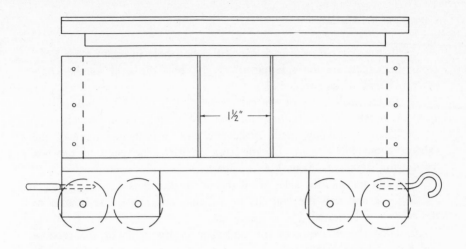

Caboose
2 pc 7/16" x 1 1/2" x 1 3/4"—ends
2 pc 7/16" x 1 1/2" x 3 1/2"—sides
1 pc 1/4" x 2 5/8" x 5"—bottom
1 pc 1/4" x 2 5/8" x 5"
1 pc 1/4" x 1 11/16" x 2 9/16"—A } roof
1 pc 3/4" x 1 1/2" x 1 5/8"—cupola
8 pc 7/8" x 2" x 2"—trucks for all cars
No. 16 brads 1" long
32—3/4" no. 6 round head screws—axles
32 wheels 1" in diameter
5 size 10 screw eyes   }
4 size 12 screw hooks } couplers

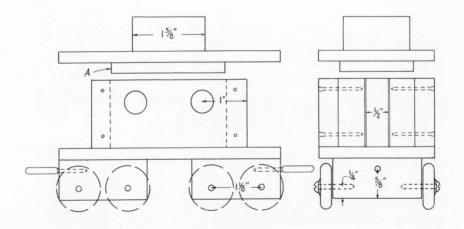

1. In the side pieces of each car drill a nail hole in each corner 1/4″ from the edges. In the side pieces of the box car drill another hole midway between the corner holes.

2. In each side piece of the caboose also drill two 1/2″ holes about 1/8″ in depth 1″ from either end and 1/2″ from the upper edge.

3. Using a thin saw blade make two cuts in each end piece of the caboose about 1/2″ apart. Do the same in each side piece of the box car spacing these cuts about 1 1/2″ apart.

4. Glue and nail the sides of all the cars to the ends.

5. Glue and nail the bottoms to the ends and sides. The bottom of the caboose will extend 3/4″ at each end.

6. Glue the A pieces to the underside of the roofs of the caboose and box car, equidistant from the end and side edges. Glue the cupola to the center of the caboose roof and the catwalk to the center of the box car roof.

7. In the ends of each truck drill two pilot holes into the end grain of the wood for the screw axles. Locate the holes 1 1/8″ apart and 1/4″ from the lower edges. Also, in one side of each truck drill a pilot hole 5/8″ up from the lower edge and centered, for the screw hook or screw eye coupler.

8. Glue a truck to the underside of each car, even with the ends and centered. Make sure that the holes for the couplers are to the outside.

9. Paint or varnish the train.

10. Install the couplers and mount the wheels.

A FREIGHT TRAIN

Materials: **Engine**

1 pc 1 1/8" x 2 1/2" x 11 1/2"—A—base
1 pc 1 1/8" x 2 1/2" x 7 1/2"—B—boiler support
2 pc 3/4" x 2 1/4" x 7 1/2"—C—boiler
2 pc 7/16" x 2 1/2" x 3"—roof, floor ⎫
2 pc 7/16" x 1 7/8" x 2 1/2"—sides ⎬ cab
1 pc 1/2" x 1 1/8" x 2 1/2"—D—rear end piece
2 single prong chair glides about 7/8" diameter—domes
1 pc 1/2" dowel 1" long—smokestack
2 furniture nails—headlight and bell
8—2" wheels
8—1 1/2" no. 10 round head screws—axles
4—1 1/4" no. 6 flat head screws
2—1 1/2" no. 6 flat head screws
4—2" no. 6 flat head screws
1 no. 10 screw hook
1" brads

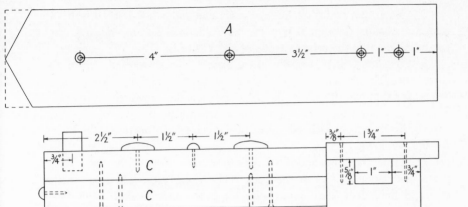

Construction: **Engine**

1. In each 1 1/8″ side of the base drill four pilot holes for the screw axles with the first hole 1 1/2″ from the rear end. Space the holes 2 1/2″ apart and 3/8″ up from the lower edge.

2. In the underside of the base, drill and countersink holes for screws 1″, 2″, 5 1/2″ and 9 1/2″ from the rear end and centered.

3. Saw off both corners of the front end of the base, with the miter gauge set at a 60 degree angle, to form the cowcatcher. Then cut off the top of the front edge at a 45 degree angle.

4. Glue the two C pieces together to make the boiler. Round off the upper side edges with the molding cutter. In the underside of the lower C piece drill and countersink holes for 1 1/4″ screws 1 1/2″ from each end and centered. Drive in the screws.

5. In the upper C piece drill a 1/2″ hole about 1/2″ in depth 3/4″ from the front end and centered for the smokestack. Also drill small pilot holes for the domes and bell 2 1/2″, 4″ and 5 1/2″ from the front end. Sand the sides and top of the boiler.

6. Sand the sides and top of the B piece rounding off the side edges slightly. In the underside of this piece drill and countersink two holes for screws. Locate the holes 2″ from each end and equidistant from the side edges.

7. Center the boiler on piece B and glue and screw it to B with 2″ screws driven up through B into the boiler. Sand the front end and drive the headlight into the center of one of the C pieces.

8. Glue the boiler assembly to the base 1″ back from the tip of the cowcatcher.

9. In the two holes in the base nearest the cowcatcher drive 2″ screws up through the base A into the boiler support B.

10. In the top of each side piece of the cab cut an opening 5/8″ x 1″ for the windows.

11. Glue the roof and floor pieces to the sides of the cab. These pieces will extend 1/2″ at the back end. Along each side edge of the roof and floor drill small pilot holes for brads 3/8″ and 2 1/8″ from the front end of these pieces. To avoid splitting the narrow sides of the windows drill the pilot holes through the roof into the side pieces. Drive in the brads.

12. Glue the cab to the base against the end of the boiler assembly. Drive two 1 1/2″ screws up through the base into the floor of the cab.

13. Glue the smokestack in the hole drilled for it and drive the domes and bell into the boiler.

14. In the D piece drill and countersink holes for screws 1/2″ from each end and centered. Also drill a hole for a screw hook in the center of the piece 3/8″ from the lower side edge. With a drill slightly larger than the shank of the hook, enlarge this center hole to a depth of 1/8″ or so. This will prevent any splintering of the wood by the threads of the hook. Glue and screw with 1 1/4″ screws the D piece to the back end of the base. Insert the screw hook through the D piece into the end of the base.

15. Apply the finish before mounting the wheels.

Materials: Tender

1 pc 3/4″ x 2 1/2″ x 6″—bottom
2 pc 3/4″ x 2 1/2″ x 2 1/2″—ends
2 pc 7/16″ x 2 1/2″ x 7 1/2″—sides

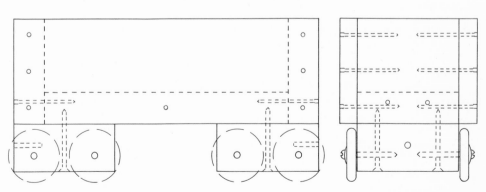

Gondola Car
1 pc 3/4″ x 2 1/2″ x 8 1/2″—bottom
2 pc 3/4″ x 2″ x 2 1/2″—ends
2 pc 7/16″ x 2″ x 10″—sides

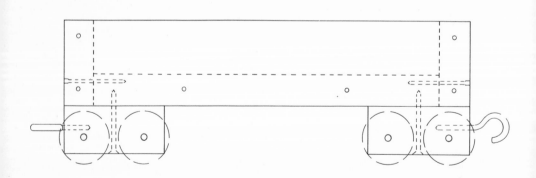

Box Car

1 pc 3/4" x 2 1/2" x 8 1/2"—bottom
2 pc 3/4" x 3" x 2 1/2"—ends
2 pc 7/16" x 3" x 10"—sides
1 pc 1/4" x 3 3/8" x 10"—A ⎫
1 pc 1/4" x 2 7/16" x 8 7/16"—B ⎬ roof
1 pc 1/16" x 3/4" x 10"—catwalk

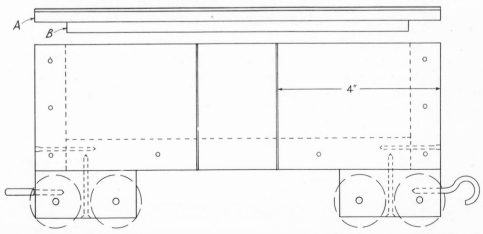

Flat Car
1 pc 3/4" x 3 1/2" x 10"

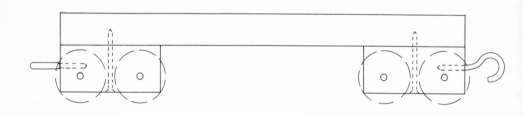

Caboose
2 pc 7/16″ x 3 1/2″ x 7″—bottom, roof
2 pc 3/4″ x 2″ x 2 1/2″—ends
2 pc 7/16″ x 2″ x 5 1/2″—sides
1 pc 1″ x 2 1/2″ x 2 1/2″—cupola
1 pc 1/4″ x 2 7/16″ x 3 15/16″—A

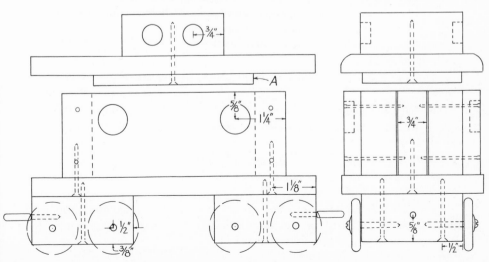

The following materials are for the five cars listed above:

10 pc 1 1/8" x 2 1/2" x 2 1/2"—trucks

40—1 1/4" wheels

40—1 1/4" no. 8 round head screws—axles

23—1 1/2" no. 6 flat head screws

6 no. 10 screw eyes ⎫
5 no. 10 screw hooks ⎬ couplers

No. 4 finishing nails

Construction: **Tender, Gondola car, Box car**

1. In each end piece drill two pilot holes for nails 3/4" from the side edges and 1/2" from the lower edge.

2. Glue and nail the end pieces to the bottom piece.

3. In the side pieces, drill holes for nails along the ends and bottom 3/8" from the edges as in the diagram. In each side piece of the box car make a vertical saw cut 4" from either end to represent a door.

4. Glue and nail the sides to the ends and bottom.

5. Make the box car roof by gluing piece B to the underside of piece A equidistant from the edges of A. Glue the catwalk to the center of the roof. The roof will be removable.

6. Sand the completed cars.

Construction: **The Caboose**

1. In each side piece drill two 3/4" holes about 1/4" in depth, 1 1/4" from the ends and 5/8" from one edge (upper), to represent windows.

2. Drill a hole for a nail in each corner of the side pieces, 3/8" from either edge.

3. In each side of the cupola, drill two 1/2" holes about 1/4" in depth 3/4" from the ends and 1/2" from the top.

4. In each end piece make two shallow, vertical saw cuts 3/4" apart to represent doors.

5. Glue and nail the sides to the ends. Sand the assembled caboose body.

6. Glue the body to the bottom 3/4" from either end and centered.

7. In the underside of the bottom drill and countersink two holes for 1 1/4" screws 1 1/8" in from each end and centered. Drive the screws through the bottom into the ends of the caboose body.

8. Round off the upper side edges of the roof

9. Glue the cupola to the center of the roof.

10. Glue the A piece to the underside of the roof equidistant from the ends and sides. Drill and countersink a hole for a screw in the center

of the underside of the A piece. Drive a screw through A, the roof and into the cupola.

Construction: The Trucks

1. In the ends of each truck drill two pilot holes into the end grain of the wood for the screw axles. Locate the holes 1/2″ from the side edges and 3/8″ from the lower surface.

2. In the center of one 1 1/8″ side drill a pilot hole for the coupler (screw hook or screw eye) 5/8″ from the lower surface. Enlarge the hole to avoid splintering the wood.

3. In the lower surface of each truck drill and countersink two holes 1/2″ from each end and centered for the screws to attach the truck to the car.

4. Glue and screw the trucks to the cars and caboose even with the ends and equidistant from the side edges. Be sure to have the holes for the couplers to the outside.

5. Varnish or paint the train.

6. Screw in the couplers and mount the wheels.

Materials: Diesel Engine

1 pc 3/4″ x 2 1/2″ x 13 1/2″—bottom
3 pc 3/4″ x 3 3/8″ x 3 1/2″—A ⎱
1 pc 3/4″ x 3 3/8″ x 1 3/4″—B ⎰ front section
2 pc 7/16″ x 3/4″ x 3 1/2″—filler—front
1 pc 3/4″ x 3″ x 2 1/2″—back end
1 pc 3/4″ x 2 1/4″ x 2 1/2″—front end
2 pc 7/16″ x 3″ x 10 3/4″—sides
1 pc 3/4″ x 3 3/8″ x 12″—roof
1 pc 1/4″ plywood 2 7/16″ x 9 3/16″—C
2 pc 1 1/8″ x 4″ x 2 1/2″—trucks
4 pc 3/8″ x 3/4″ x 1 3/8″—fillers—D
8—1 1/4″ wheels
8—1 1/4″ no. 8 round head screws—axles
8—1 1/2″ no. 6 flat head screws
1 furniture nail—headlight
1 no. 10 screw hook—coupler
No. 4 finishing nails
No. 6 finishing nails

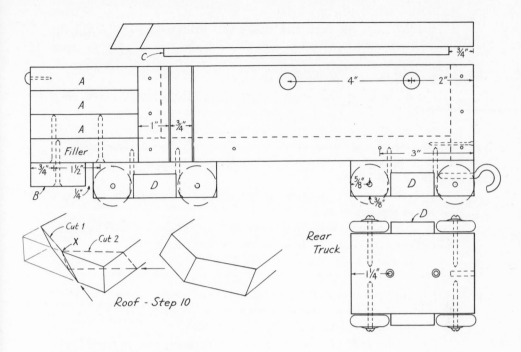

Roof - Step 10

Rear Truck

Construction: Diesel Engine

1. Glue one of the front filler pieces to each side of the bottom and even with one end (front).

2. Glue the three A pieces together. Then glue them to the front end of the bottom and filler pieces. Drill and countersink two holes in the underside of the bottom 3/4″ and 2 1/4″ from the front end and centered. Drive two 1 1/2″ screws up through the bottom into the A pieces or front section of the engine.

3. Drill and countersink two holes for screws in piece B 3/4″ from the side edges and centered. Glue and screw the piece to the underside of the bottom and filler pieces even with the front end.

4. Round off the front side edges of this assembly on the sander.

5. Drive the headlight into the center of the upper A piece.

6. In the back end piece, drill two pilot holes for no. 6 nails 1/2″ in from the side edges and 1/2″ from the lower edge. Glue and nail the piece to the end of the bottom.

7. Glue the front end piece against the back end of the front section 7/16″ from each side edge and even with the top of the end section.

8. In the corners of each side piece drill pilot holes for nails 3/8″ in from the edges. Also, drill a hole midway between the corner holes. Along the lower side edges drill pilot holes for nails 3″ from the front and rear ends and 3/8″ from the lower edges. Also drill 1/2″ holes about 1/4″ in depth 1/2″ from the upper edge of each side piece and

145

2" and 6" from the back end. Make two shallow saw cuts across the grain 1" from the front end of each side and about 3/4" apart to represent doors.

9. Nail the sides to the ends and bottom.

10. Make a mark X at the center of one surface of the roof piece and shape the front end of the roof as follows:

a. With the saw tilted at 30 degrees and the miter gauge set at 60 degrees saw off one corner of the end to point X. Two or three passes of the piece through the saw may be necessary so the cut is made exactly to point X. See diagram.

b. Turn the miter gauge to 60 degrees on the other side of center and repeat the operation.

Or, saw one end of the roof piece with the saw tilted at 30 degrees and make a straight slanted front instead of the pointed one.

11. Round off the upper side edges of the roof with the molding cutter.

12. Glue piece C to the underside of the roof slightly more than 3/4" from the rear end and equidistant from the side edges. The roof will fit into the top of the engine and will be removable.

13. In the ends of each truck, drill pilot holes into the end grain of the wood for the axles. Locate the holes 5/8" from the side edges and 3/8" from the lower surface.

14. In one truck (rear) drill a hole for the coupler 5/8" from the lower edge and centered. With a drill a little larger than the shank of the screw hook enlarge the hole to a depth of 1/8" or so to avoid splintering the wood when the coupler is inserted.

15. Drill and countersink two holes for screws in the lower side of each truck 1 1/4" from the side edges and centered.

16. Glue and screw the front truck to the underside of the base about 1/4" back from piece B and the rear truck in place even with the back end of the engine with the hole for the coupler to the back. Screw in the coupler.

17. Glue the filler pieces D to the ends of the trucks centered between the holes for the axles and even with the lower edge of the trucks.

18. Apply the finish before mounting the wheels.

Materials: **Baggage Car**

1 pc 3/4" x 2 1/2" x 10 1/2"—bottom
2 pc 3/4" x 2 1/2" x 2 1/4"—ends
2 pc 7/16" x 3" x 10 1/2"—sides
1 pc 7/16" x 3 3/8" x 10 1/2"   ⎫
1 pc 1/4" x 2 7/16" x 8 15/16"—A ⎬ roof
2 pc 1 1/8" x 2 1/2" x 2 1/2"—trucks
8—1 1/4" wheels
8—1 1/4" no. 8 round head screws
4—1 1/2" flat head screws
1 no. 10 screw hook ⎫
1 no. 10 screw eye ⎬ coupler
No. 4 finishing nails

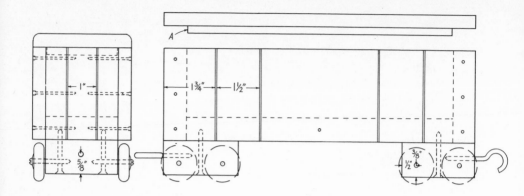

Construction: **Baggage Car**

1. In each end piece make shallow saw cuts lengthwise with the grain of the wood 1″ apart to represent doors.

2. In each side piece make shallow saw cuts across the grain 1 3/4″ from each end and 1 1/2″ apart to represent doors.

3. Glue the ends to the bottom even with the front and back edges of the bottom.

4. In the side pieces drill pilot holes for nails in each corner 3/8″ in from the edges. Also drill a hole at the ends and lower edge midway between these holes.

5. Nail the sides to the ends and bottom.

6. In the ends of the trucks drill pilot holes into the end grain for the screw axles 1/2″ from the side edges and 3/8″ from the lower edges.

7. In one side of each truck drill a pilot hole for the coupler 5/8″ from the lower edge and centered. Enlarge these holes to a depth of 1/8″ or so to avoid splintering the wood when the coupler is inserted.

8. In the lower surface of each truck drill and countersink two holes 1 1/4″ from the front and back edges, and 1/2″ from the ends for the 1 1/2″ screws to attach the trucks to the car.

9. Glue the trucks in place even with the ends of the bottom and centered. Be sure the holes for the couplers are to the outside. Drive in the screws.

10. Round off the side edges of the roof on the sander or with the molding cutter. Glue piece A to the underside of the roof equidistant from the end and side edges.

11. Apply the finish.

12. Screw in the couplers and mount the wheels.

Materials: **Passenger Car**

1 pc 3/4" x 2 1/2" x 9 3/4"—bottom
2 pc 3/4" x 2 1/2" x 2 1/4"—ends
2 pc 7/16" x 1 1/2" x 9 3/4"—A ⎫
2 pc 7/16" x 3/4" x 9 3/4"—B ⎬ sides
2 pc 1/8" plastic 1" x 10" ⎭
1 pc 7/16" x 3 3/8" x 12" ⎫ roof
1 pc 1/4" x 2 7/16" x 8 3/16"—C ⎭
2 pc 1 1/8" x 3 3/8" x 3"—front, rear sections
2 pc 1 1/8" x 2 1/2" x 2 1/2"—trucks
8—1 1/4" wheels
8—1 1/4" no. 8 round head screws
4—2" no. 6 flat head screws
4—1 1/2" no. 6 flat head screws
1 no. 10 screw hook—coupler
1 no. 10 screw eye—coupler
No. 4 finishing nails

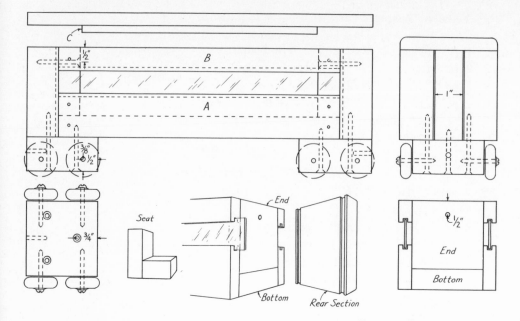

Construction: **Passenger Car**

1. In each end piece drill and countersink a hole for a screw 1/2″ from the top edge and equidistant from the side edges.

2. Glue the ends to the bottom even with the front and back edges of the bottom with the holes up and to the inside.

3. Saw a groove lengthwise about 1/8″ in depth along the center of one edge of each of the side pieces. The grooves should be wide enough so that the plastic will slide through them. Also, in the front and rear sections make two similar vertical grooves in the inside surfaces about 1/8″ in from the side edges. The ends of the windows will fit into these grooves so no edges will be exposed.

4. In the outside surfaces of the front and rear end sections, make shallow saw cuts 1 1/8″ in from the side edges to represent doors.

5. In each corner of side piece A drill pilot holes for nails 3/8″ in from the edges. In each side piece B drill a similar hole 3/8″ from each end and centered.

6. Glue and nail the sides in place even with the lower edge of the bottom and the upper edge of the ends. A 3/4″ wide space will be left between the side pieces for the windows.

7. Glue the front end section to the assembled car making sure that the grooves in the sides and front section meet. Drive a 1 1/2″ screw through the end of the car into the front end section.

8. In the ends of the trucks, drill pilot holes into the end grain for the screw axles 1/2″ from the side edges and 3/8″ from the lower edges.

150

9. In one side of each truck drill a pilot hole for the coupler 5/8" from the lower edge and centered. Enlarge these holes to a depth of 1/8" or so to avoid splintering the wood when the couplers are inserted.

10. Each truck for the passenger car has three holes drilled and countersunk for the screws to attach it to the car. The two holes nearest the sides where the holes for the couplers are located are 1/2" in from the ends and 3/4" from the side edges. The third hole is 3/4" from the inner side edge and centered. When gluing the trucks to the car be sure to have the holes for the couplers to the outside or to the front and rear of the car.

11. Glue the front truck to the bottom and front end section even with the front edge. Drive 2" screws through the truck into the end section and a 1 1/2" screw through the truck into the bottom.

12. Glue the rear truck to the bottom letting it extend 1 1/8" beyond the end of the bottom to allow for the thickness of the rear end section when that is put in place.

13. Round off the top side edges of the roof. Center piece C on the underside of the roof and glue it in place.

14. Before proceeding further apply finish to all parts.

15. Slide the windows into the grooves.

16. Glue and screw the rear section in place against the end piece and on the truck. Drive the screws through the truck into the end section and bottom.

17. Mount the wheels and screw in the couplers.

If seats are made for the car the backs should be 1/4" x 1" x 1 1/4" and the seat part 7/16" x 1" x 3/4".

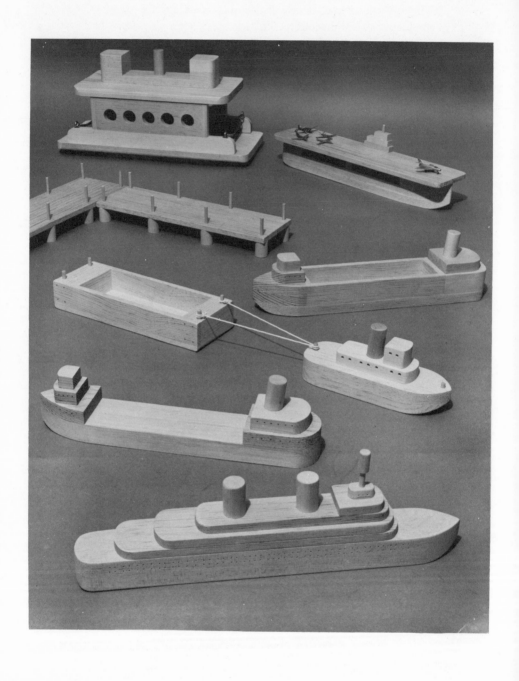

Section 6

A Tugboat and Barge
A Freighter
A Great Lakes Cargo Ship
An Ocean Liner
A Ferry Boat
An Aircraft Carrier
A Wharf

A TUGBOAT AND BARGE

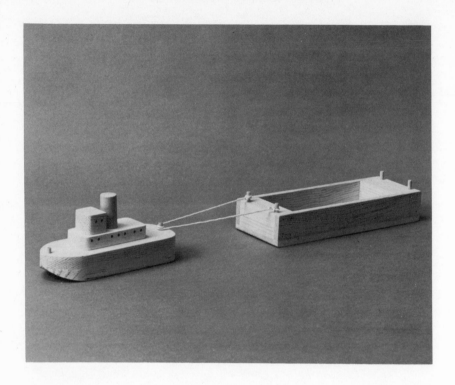

Materials: Tugboat

2 pc 3/4" x 3 1/4" x 10"—hull
1 pc 3/4" x 2" x 5"—deckhouse
1 pc 1 1/8" x 1 1/2" x 1 1/2"—pilothouse
1 pc 1" dowel 2" long—smokestack
2 pc 1/4" dowel 1" long—posts (bitts)

Construction: Tugboat

1. Glue the two sections of the hull together and shape as shown. Plates or cans can be used to draw the curves for the hull, deckhouse and pilothouse. For example, a 7" plate can be used for the two curved edges of the bow and a 5 3/4" saucer as a guide for the stern.

2. Drill a 1/4" hole about 1/2" deep 5/8" from each end and centered, for the bitts.

154

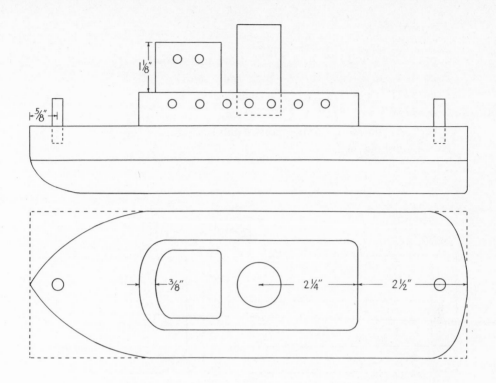

3. In each side of the deckhouse drill seven 3/16″ holes about 1/4″ in depth. Locate the two holes at each end 3/4″ and 1 1/4″ from the ends. Drill one hole in the center with holes 1/2″ to either side of the center hole. The holes are up 1/2″ from the lower edge of the deckhouse.

4. Drill a 1″ hole about 1/2″ deep 2 1/4″ from one end (stern) of the deckhouse and centered, for the smokestack.

5. Round off one end (front) of the pilothouse and drill two 3/16″ holes about 1/2″ apart in each side and 3/8″ from top edge.

6. Glue the pilot house to the deckhouse about 3/8″ from the front end and centered.

7. Glue this assembly to the hull 2 1/2″ from the stern and centered. If the boat is to be used in water, instead of or as well as a floor toy, be sure that the upper structure is equidistant from the side edges. Some experimenting in placement of deckhouse may be necessary so that the boat will ride evenly in the water. Also, it will be necessary to use a water proof glue.

Materials: **Barge**

2 pc 3/4" x 1 1/2" x 3 1/2"—front end (bow)
2 pc 3/4" x 2" x 3 1/2"—back end (stern)
2 pc 7/16" x 1 1/2" x 12"—sides
1 pc 7/16" x 4 3/8" x 12"—bottom
4 pc 1/4" dowel 1" long—posts (bitts)
No. 4 finishing nails

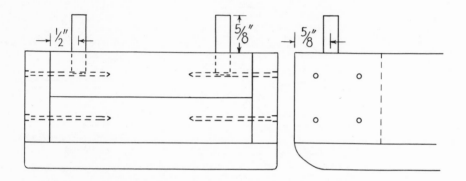

Construction: **Barge**

1. Glue the two pieces together to form the bow; do the same for the stern.

2. Drill 1/4" holes 3/8" in depth in top surface of bow and stern for the bitts. Locate the holes in the bow 5/8" from the front edge and 1/2" in from either end. The holes in the stern are also 1/2" in from either end and 5/8" from the back edge of that piece.

3. Glue and nail the side pieces to the end sections of the bow and stern using 4 nails at each end. Locate the nails 3/8" in from the edges of the sides and about 3/4" apart.

4. Glue and nail on the bottom.

5. Drive the bitts into the holes.

6. Paint or varnish the barge and tugboat.

When the barge is being towed attach it to the tugboat with a hawser (cord) as in the photograph.

A FREIGHTER

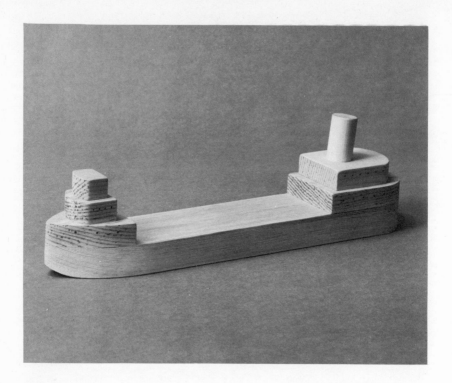

Materials:

1 pc 1 1/8″ x 3″ x 16″—hull
1 pc 3/4″ x 3″ x 3″—A—bow deck
1 pc 3/4″ x 1 3/4″ x 1 1/2″—B—officer's quarters
1 pc 3/4″ x 1 1/4″ x 1″—C—pilot house
1 pc 3/4″ x 3″ x 4″—D—stern deck
1 pc 3/4″ x 2 1/2″ x 3″—E—engineering crew's quarters
1 pc 1″ dowel 2 1/4″ long—smokestack

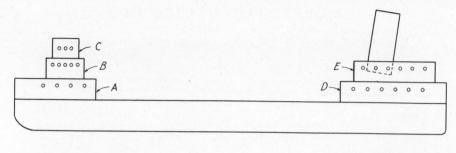

Construction:

1. Glue the A piece to one end of the hull and the D piece to the other end.

2. Shape the hull as shown in the diagram. One way to get the pointed bow is to locate the exact center of the A piece and using a medium size plate or large can top draw lines from the center to the back corners of the A piece. A cup or large glass can be used to get the rounded stern. Round off underside of the bow.

3. Round off one end of the E piece (back). Drill a 1″ hole at a slight slant about 1/2″ in depth 2″ from the same end.

4. Insert the smokestack into the hole and glue E to D.

5. Round off one end (front) of the B and C pieces. Glue B to A and C to B.

6. Small holes (about 1/16″) may be drilled or made with an awl or nail for portholes in pieces A,B,C,D, and E as seen in the diagram.

7. Paint or varnish the ship.

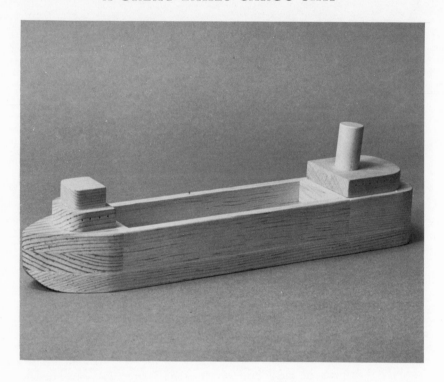

Materials:

1 pc 3/4" x 3 1/2" x 18"—A ⎫
2 pc 3/4" x 3 1/2" x 3 1/2"—B ⎪
2 pc 3/4" x 3 1/2" x 4"—C ⎬ hull
2 pc 7/16" x 1 1/2" x 2 5/8"—D ⎪
2 pc 7/16" x 1 1/2" x 10 1/2"—E ⎭
1 pc 3/4" x 2 1/4" x 2"—F—officer's quarters
1 pc 3/4" x 1 1/2" x 1 1/2"—G—pilothouse
1 pc 3/4" x 3" x 3 1/4"—H—engineering crew's quarters
1 pc 1" dowel 2 1/4" long—smokestack

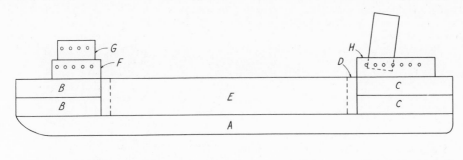

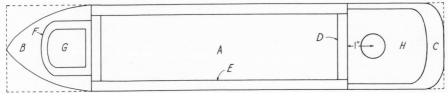

Construction:

1. Glue the B pieces together and also the C pieces. Glue the B pieces to one end of A (bow) and the C pieces to the other end (stern).

2. Shape the ends of the hull as shown.

3. Glue the D pieces to the inside ends of the bow and stern sections 7/16″ from the side edges.

4. Glue the sides (E) to the ends (D) to form a box.

5. Round off one end of the H piece (back). Drill a 1″ hole 1/2″ in depth at a slight slant 1″ from the other end and insert the smokestack. Glue the H piece to the stern section even with front edge of stern.

6. Round off one end of the F and G pieces. Glue G to F and then glue this assembly to the bow section of the ship even with back edge of bow.

7. Small holes (1/16″) can be punched or drilled as seen in diagram for portholes in pieces F, G and H.

8. Paint or varnish the ship.

9. If this ship is to be used in the water glue a 1/4″ x 1/4″ x 9 5/8″ strip on the inside of the hull along each side to cover seam between side and bottom. Also, use waterproof glue throughout.

AN OCEAN LINER

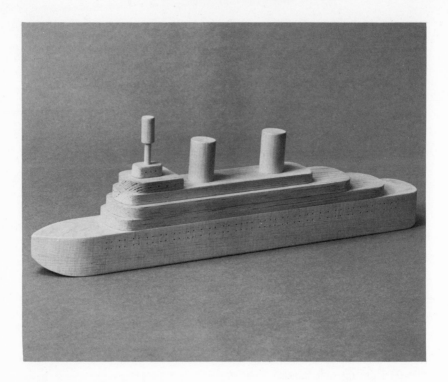

Materials:

2 pc 3/4" x 2 1/4" x 18"—hull
1 pc 7/16" x 2 1/4" x 13"—A ⎫
1 pc 7/16" x 2 1/4" x 11"—B ⎪
1 pc 7/16" x 1 3/4" x 9"—C ⎬ Superstructure
1 pc 7/16" x 1 3/4" x 2 1/4"—wheelhouse ⎭
1 pc 1/2" dowel 3/4" long ⎫
1 pc 1/4" dowel 1 1/2" long ⎬ radar tower
1 pc 7/16" x 3/4" x 1 1/4"—D (base) ⎭
2 pc 1" dowel 2" long—smokestacks
2—1 1/4" no. 6 flat head screws
2—2" no. 6 flat head screws

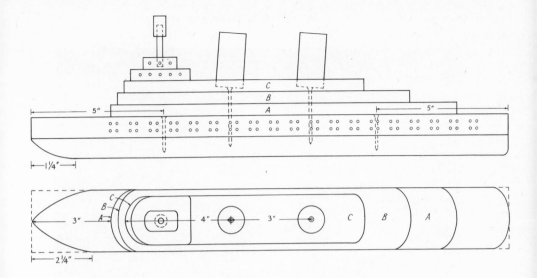

Construction:

1. Glue the two pieces for the hull together and shape as shown. Drill and countersink holes and drive the 1 1/4" screws into the hull 5" from each end and centered.

2. Round off both ends of the decks (A,B,C) and one end (front) of the wheelhouse.

3. Glue the three decks together locating B 1/4" back from the bow end of A and C 1/4" back from the bow end of B.

4. Drill two 1" holes 1/2" in depth at a 10-15 degree angle for the smokestacks 4" and 7" from the bow end of the upper deck C.

5. Glue the wheelhouse to the upper deck 1/4" from the bow end of deck C.

6. Glue the superstructure to the hull about 3" from the bow.

7. Drive the 2" screws down through the center of the 1" holes for the smokestacks into the hull. Glue the smokestacks in place.

8. Round off both ends of the D piece and drill a 1/4" hole about 3/8" in depth in the center. Drill a 1/4" hole 3/8" in depth lengthwise in the center of the 3/4" piece of dowel. Insert the 1/4" dowel into this hole to make the radar tower. Then insert the tower into the hole drilled in the base (D). Mount the radar tower gluing it about 1/2" from front edge of wheelhouse.

9. Portholes about 1/16" in diameter can be drilled or punched along the sides of the hull, the wheelhouse and the base of the radar tower.

10. Paint or varnish the ship.

A FERRY BOAT

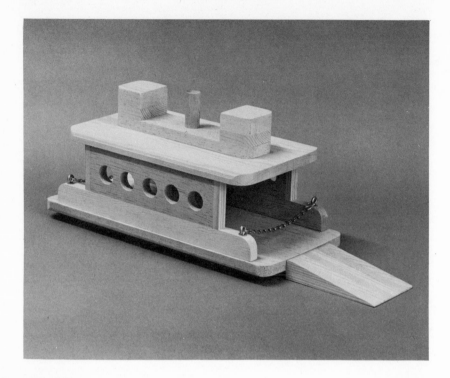

Materials:

1 pc 3/4″ x 9 1/4″ x 20″—hull
1 pc 3/4″ x 9 1/4″ x 16″—roof
2 pc 3/4″ x 3 1/4″ x 11″—A ⎫
2 pc 3/4″ x 1 1/2″ x 18″—B ⎬ sides
4 pc 1/2″ x 3/4″ x 3 1/4″—C—end posts
2 pc 3/4″ x 1″ x 11″—D—roof supports
1 pc 3/4″ x 3″ x 12″—E ⎫
2 pc 1 3/4″ x 3″ x 2 1/2″—F ⎬ pilothouse assembly
2 pc 1/2″ x 3/4″ x 18″—runners (hardwood)
1 pc 1/4″ plywood 7 1/2″ x 11″—ceiling
1 pc 1″ dowel 3″ long—smokestack
4 pc 1/4″ dowel 2 1/2″ long
4 no. 10 screw eyes
4 small S hooks
2 pc chain about 7 1/2″ long
6—1″ no. 6 flat head screws—for runners
26—1 1/2″ no. 6 flat head screws

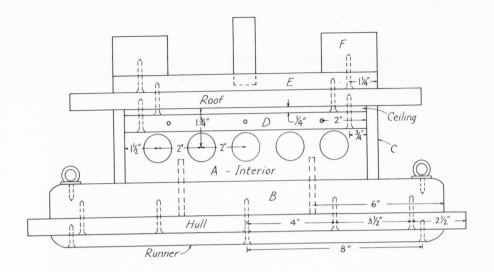

Construction:

1. In each side piece A drill five 1 1/4" holes with the centers 1 3/4" from one edge (upper) and 2" apart. Locate the center of the first hole 1 1/2" from the end.

2. In the top edge of each side piece B, drill a hole for a screw eye 1" from each end and centered. Round off the upper corner of each of these pieces.

3. Center section A on B and glue. To strengthen the sides drill holes for the 1/4" dowels up through B into A 6" from each end of B. Drive in the dowels. Or, 2 1/2" screws can be used instead of dowels.

4. Glue the posts to the ends of the A pieces.

5. Drill and countersink five holes for screws in each D piece as follows: In the 1" wide surface drill a hole 3/4" from each end and centered; then, along the center of the 3/4" wide surface drill 3 holes, 2" from each end and one in the center.

6. Glue and screw the D pieces to the inside of each A piece 1/4" down from the upper edge and with the 3/4" surface against the side.

7. Drill holes in the plywood to coincide with the holes near the ends of the D pieces, or 3/4" from the ends and 1/2" from the side edges. It is a good plan to make these holes a little larger than those in D.

8. Glue the plywood ceiling between the sides and to the upper surface of the roof supports D.

9. Along each side edge of the hull drill and countersink holes for screws 1/2" from the edge, 2 1/2" and 6" from the ends and one in the center.

10. Round off the corners of the hull and the roof. Also round off the upper side edges of the roof with the molding cutter. The bottom

side edges of the hull should also be rounded off a little but not enough to interfere with the holes for screws.

11. Glue the side assembly to the underside of the roof 2″ from the ends and 1/8″ from the side edges. Drive the screws through the D pieces into the roof.

12. Round off the ends of the runners. Drill and countersink three holes spaced about 8″ apart in each runner. Glue and screw the runners to the underside of the hull 1″ from the side edges.

13. Drill and countersink holes for screws 1 1/2″ from the ends of the plywood ceiling and centered. These screws will go up through the roof into the pilothouse assembly.

14. Drill a 1″ hole for the smokestack in the center of the E piece.

15. Sand one end (back) of each F piece and the upper surface of the E piece. Glue the F pieces to E even with the ends of E and with sanded sides toward center of E.

16. Round off the ends of the E and F pieces and finish sanding.

17. In each end of E drill and countersink two holes for screws 1 1/4″ in from end and about 3/4″ in from side edges. Drive two screws up through E into each F piece.

18. Center the pilothouse assembly on the roof and glue. Drive two screws up through screw holes in the ceiling and roof into the pilothouse assembly. Install smokestack.

19. Paint or varnish both assemblies.

20. Glue the top assembly to the hull equidistant from the ends and sides. Drive screws through the hull into the sides.

21. Install the screw eyes and attach the chain so that one end can be unhooked.

Materials: **Ramps**

2 pc 3/4″ x 1 1/8″ x 4″
2 pc 1/4″ plywood 4″ x 6″
4 pc 3/8″ x 3/4″ x 6″

Construction: **Ramps**

1. Saw off one edge of the 3/4″ stock at about a 15 degree angle. Glue the plywood to it.

2. Glue the railing along each side with the 3/8″ surface down.

Ramps may also be made by gluing six or more pieces together, and then finishing on the sander. To cut the pieces for the ramp a jig will be needed. See diagram. Saw a piece of 3/4″ stock to a length of 7″. The piece should be wide enough to make several sections of the ramp. Push it through the saw using the jig so that the small end will be about 1/8″ thick. Turn the piece over and repeat the operation. Make at least twelve sections for the two ramps.

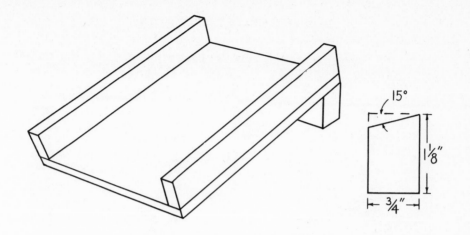

15°

1⅛"

¾"

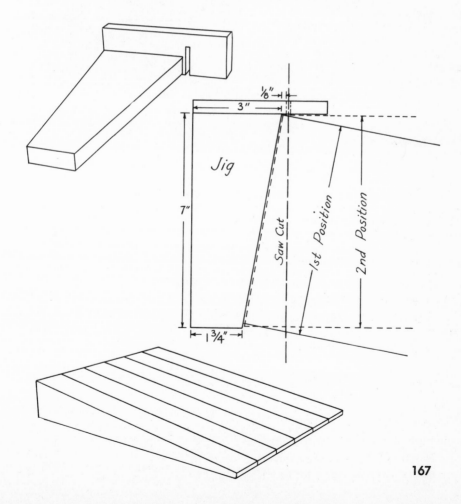

⅛"

3"

Jig

7"

Saw Cut

1st Position

2nd Position

1¾"

AN AIRCRAFT CARRIER

Materials:

2 pc 3/4″ x 2 1/2″ x 20″—A
1 pc 1 1/8″ x 2 1/2″ x 5″—B } hull
1 pc 1 1/8″ x 2 1/2″ x 3″—C

1 pc 7/16″ x 5″ x 20″
       or } flight deck
1 pc 1/4″ x 5″ x 20″

1 pc 3/4″ x 1 1/8″ x 2 1/2″—deck support

1 pc 1/2″ x 3/4″ x 3″
1 pc 1/2″ x 3/4″ x 2 1/2″ } island
1 pc 1/2″ x 3/4″ x 1 1/2″
1 pc 1/4″ dowel 1″ long

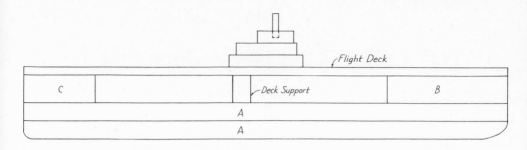

Construction:

1. Glue the two A pieces together.

2. Glue the B piece to the bow and the C piece to the stern.

3. Shape the hull as shown in the diagram. A 10″ plate can be used to get the shape of the bow while a 4″ cup can be used to shape the stern. Round off bottoms of bow and stern.

4. Glue the deck support midway between pieces B and C.

5. Round off the corners of the flight deck and glue it to pieces B, C and deck support.

6. Assemble the island. Drill a 1/4″ hole in the center of the upper piece for the dowel.

7. Glue the island to the port side midway between the ends of the deck.

8. Paint or varnish the ship.

A WHARF

Materials: (for one section)

1 pc 7/16" x 5" x 16"
8 pc 1" dowel 1 1/4" long
8 pc 1/4" dowel 2 1/4" long

Construction:

1. Drill a 1/4" hole about 1/2" in depth in the center of each of the 1" dowels.

2. Drive the 1/4" dowels into these holes.

3. Drill four 17/64" holes along each side. Locate the first hole 1/2" from one end and the others 5" apart. The holes are 1/2" in from the side edges. By making 17/64" holes the posts can be removed and the wharf disassembled. If it is not to be taken apart, use a 1/4" drill instead of 17/64".

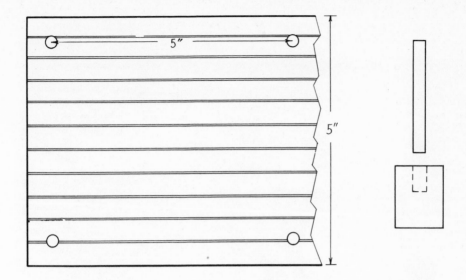

4. Shallow grooves made with a thin saw blade can be cut lengthwise in the upper side to resemble planks.

5. Paint or varnish the wharf and set it on the posts. By making three or more sections of the wharf, interesting combinations can be arranged as in the photograph.

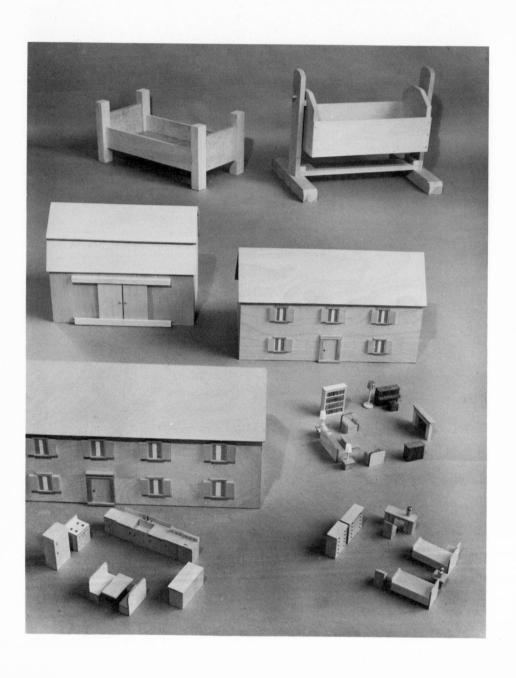

Section 7

A SALTBOX DOLL HOUSE
(FOUR ROOMS)

Materials:

1 pc 3/4″ x 10″ x 17 3/4″—first floor
3 pc 3/4″ x 11″ x 10″—ends, partition
1 pc 1/4″ x 7 1/2″ x 10 1/4″—floor—bedroom
1 pc 1/4″ x 7 1/2″ x 7 1/4″—floor—bathroom
1 pc 1/4″ x 6″ x 19 3/4″—roof—front
1 pc 1/4″ x 1 1/2″ x 19 3/4″ ⎫
1 pc 1/4″ x 8″ x 19 3/4″ ⎭ roof—back
1 pc 1/4″ x 7 1/8″ x 19 1/4″—front
5 pc 1/16″ x 1 1/2″ x 2 1/2″—A—backs
10 pc 1/8″ x 3/4″ x 1 1/2″—B—fillers
10 pc 1/16″ x 5/8″ x 1 1/2″—C—shutters
5 pc 1/8″ x 1/4″ x 1 3/8″—sills   ⎬ window assemblies
5 pc 3/16″ x 1/4″ x 1 3/8″—tops
5 pc heavy paper 1 1/8″ x 1 1/2″ ⎫
5 pc plastic 1 1/8″ x 1 1/2″   ⎭ windows

1 pc 1/8" x 1 1/2" x 2 1/2"—door ⎫
2 pc 1/4" x 3/8" x 2 1/2"—sides ⎪
1 pc 1/4" x 3/8" x 2 1/4"—X ⎫⎪
1 pc 1/8" x 3/8" x 2 1/4"—Y ⎬top ⎬ door assembly
1 pc 1/4" x 3/8" x 2 1/4"—sill ⎭⎪
1 small brass screw or nail—knob ⎭
6—2" no. 6 flat head screws
3—1 1/2" no. 6 flat head screws
3—3/4" brass butt hinges
No. 18—1 1/4" brads

Construction:

1. Across the top 10" edge of one end draw a line 3 1/2" from one side edge using the try square as a guide.

2. Set the miter gauge at 45 degrees and, with the stop on the gauge against the lower end of the piece being sawed, make cut 1 starting at the line. Make a similar cut in the other end and the partition. The stop will have to be moved before making cut 2. Turn the pieces over and make cut 2 starting at the same line.

3. In the inside surface of each end section cut grooves slightly more than 1/4" wide and about 3/16" deep and 4 3/4" from the lower edge. Cut similar grooves in each side of the partition.

4. Saw a 3/4" strip off the lower edge of the partition. Be sure to include the thickness of the saw blade when making the 3/4" measurement.

5. In the outside of each end section drill and countersink three holes for screws 3/8" from the lower edge. Locate one hole in the center and the others 1" from either end.

6. In the underside of the floor drill and countersink three holes for screws 10 3/8" from one end to fasten the partition in place. Locate the holes 1" from front and back edges and one centered between these two.

7. Glue and screw the ends to the floor using the 2" screws. Glue the partition to the floor, centered on the holes, and drive in the screws.

8. Nail on the front roof piece allowing it to extend 1/4" over the peak of each end section and 1/4" beyond the ends.

9. Fasten the two rear roof pieces together with the hinges. Locate the hinges about 1" from the ends and one in the center. Nail the 1 1/2" section of this roof assembly to the ends and partition.

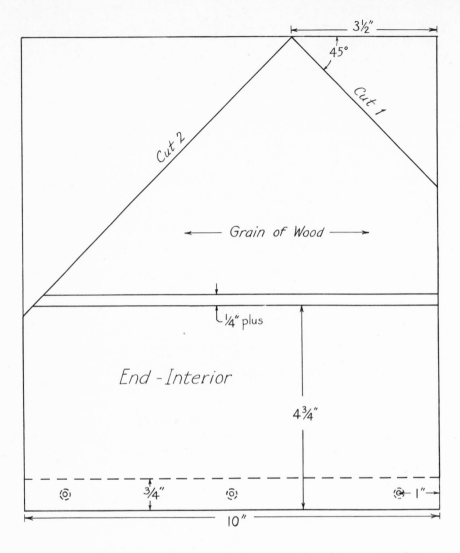

3½"

45°

Cut 1

Cut 2

← Grain of Wood →

¼" plus

End - Interior

4¾"

¾"

1"

10"

10. It is best to assemble the windows and glue them to the front of the house before the front is fastened on. Along one edge of each filler piece B make a saw cut about 1/32" deep and 1/16" in width. Glue the filler pieces to the back A, even with the side edges and with the saw cuts on the underside. The window will fit into these saw cuts.

Glue a shutter to each filler piece so it is even with the outer edges or so that 1/8" of piece B is exposed. This exposed part is the side piece of the window frame.

11. Cut pieces of heavy white paper or light cardboard 1 1/8" x 1 1/2" or so they will fit between the saw cuts made in the B pieces.

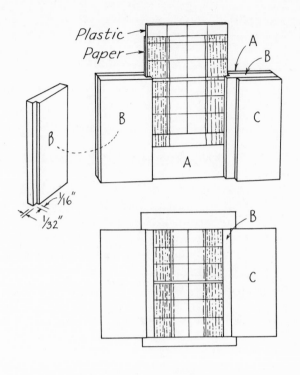

Plastic
Paper

A
B

B

B

C

A

1/16"
1/32"

B

C

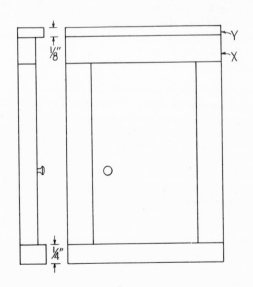

Y

X

1/8"

O

1/4"

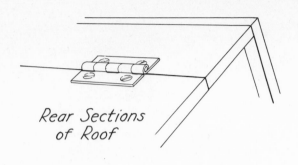

Rear Sections of Roof

Color draperies 3/8" wide along each side of the paper or cardboard. Or, use a colored tape.

12. To make window panes draw lines with a sharp tool on thin plastic. Use a larger piece of plastic than the window and cut it to size (1 1/8" x 1 1/2") after marking the panes. An easy way to do this is to fasten the plastic with tape over squared graph paper and use the lines as guides. Paper with 1/4" squares will make 24 panes in each window. Slide the windows into the frames.

13. If the house is to be painted, it should be done before installing the windows.

14. Drive a small brass screw or nail into the door about 1 1/8" up from the bottom for the knob. Glue the door to the front of the house 1/2" from the lower edge and centered. Glue the side frame pieces in place. Glue the door sill to the house with the 1/4" side against the house. Glue the X piece above the door with the 3/8" surface against the house and the Y piece to the X piece with the 1/8" surface against the house. The Y piece will then extend over the X piece.

15. Glue the window assemblies to the front of the house. The first floor windows are 1 1/4" from the lower edge of the front and 3" from the ends. The second floor windows are 3/4" from the upper edge and directly above the first floor windows. The middle window is above the door and in the center of the front of the house.

16. Glue the top frame pieces over the windows with the 1/4" sides against the house. Glue the sills below the windows with the 1/8" side against the house.

17. Nail the front to the ends and partition.

18. Slide the upper floors into the grooves.

A SALTBOX DOLL HOUSE
(SIX ROOMS)

Materials:

1 pc 3/4" x 10" x 25"—first floor

4 pc 3/4" x 11" x 10"—ends, partitions

1 pc 1/4" x 7 1/2" x 9 3/4"—floor—master bedroom

2 pc 1/4" x 7 1/2" x 7 1/4"—floors—children's room, bathroom

1 pc 1/4" x 6" x 27"—roof—front

1 pc 1/4" x 1 1/2" x 27" ⎫
1 pc 1/4" x 8" x 27"   ⎬ roof—back

1 pc 1/4" x 7 1/8" x 26 1/2"—front of house

9 pc 1/16" x 1 1/2" x 2 1/2"—A—backs ⎫

18 pc 1/8" x 3/4" x 1 1/2"—B—fillers   ⎪

18 pc 1/16" x 5/8" x 1 1/2"—C—shutters ⎪ window

9 pc 1/8" x 1/4" x 1 3/8"—sills ⎫frames ⎬ assemblies

9 pc 3/16" x 1/4" x 1 3/8"—tops ⎭   ⎪

9 pc heavy white paper 1 1/8" x 1 1/2" ⎫windows ⎪

9 pc plastic 1 1/8" x 1 1/2"   ⎭   ⎭

1 pc 1/8" x 1 1/2" x 2 1/2"—door

2 pc 1/4" x 3/8" x 2 1/2"—sides ⎫

1 pc 1/4" x 3/8" x 2 1/4"—X ⎫   ⎬ frame for door

1 pc 1/8" x 3/8" x 2 1/4"—Y ⎭ top   ⎪

1 pc 1/4" x 3/8" x 2 1/2"—sill ⎭

6—2" no. 6 flat head screws

6—1 1/2" no. 6 flat head screws

4—1" brass butt hinges

1 small round head brass screw or nail—door knob

No. 18—1 1/4" brads

The 6 room house is constructed the same as the 4 room house with the following exceptions:

1. The holes drilled in the underside of the floor for the partitions are 9 7/8" from one end, for the living room, and 17 5/8" from the same end for the kitchen.

2. The first floor windows are 1 1/4" from the lower edge of the front and 2 1/4" and 7 1/2" from the ends. The second floor windows are 3/4" from the upper edge and directly above the first floor windows. The middle window is above the door and in the center of the front of the house.

3. To fasten the two rear roof pieces together locate a hinge 1" from either end and the other two hinges 9" from either end or 7" apart.

181

The doors and drawers can be outlined with a sharp knife, razor blade, sharp tool such as an awl, or with a thin circular saw blade or coping saw. Or, pieces can be butted together to give the appearance of doors. If this is done, break the edges with sandpaper before gluing.

When no. 1 paper clips are used for handles drill the pilot holes 1/4" apart. Cut pieces 1/4" to 3/8" long from the curved ends of the clips.

Pins with colored heads or common pins, brass escutcheon pins or small nails can be used for knobs on the furniture. Cut pieces 1/4" to 3/8" long from the head end of the pins and drive them into pilot holes drilled in the furniture. The approximate location of the knobs and handles is shown in the diagrams.

Plastic caps from toothpaste and shaving cream tubes or small bottles make good lamp shades.

Plywood 1/4", 1/8" or 1/16" thick, which can be purchased at a hobby store, is very good for parts of the furniture and for the window assemblies of the doll house.

The inside walls of the doll house may be painted or papered to suit the builder, or more important, to suit the little girl who will play with the house. Old wallpaper books can often be obtained at a store where wallpaper is sold. Or, a self-adhesive plastic can be used.

The furniture and appliances can be painted, varnished or shellacked depending on the wood used. For example, if a piece of walnut or maple were used for a piece of furniture that piece should probably not be painted.

The floors may be covered with some material or painted. Pictures may be pasted to thin pieces of plywood or cardboard and fastened to the walls.

THE LIVING ROOM

Materials: The Fireplace

1 pc 1/8″ x 2″ x 3″—back
1 pc 1/8″ x 5/8″ x 3 1/4″—mantle
1 pc 3/8″ x 1/2″ x 3″—lintel
2 pc 3/8″ x 1/2″ x 1 1/2″—sides

Construction:

    1. Glue the lintel to the back even with one edge (upper).
    2. Glue the sides to the back and underside of lintel.
    3. Round off the front corners of the mantle and glue it to the upper edge of the lintel.

Materials: Bookcase

2 pc 3/16″ x 1/2″ x 3″—ends
2 pc 3/16″ x 1/2″ x 2″—cross braces
1 pc 1/8″ x 11/16″ x 2 3/8″—top
3 pc 3/32″ (or thickness of saw blade) x 1/2″ x 2 1/4″—shelves
1 pc 1/8″ x 3″ x 2 3/8″—back

Construction:

1. Make saw cuts for the shelves in each end piece spaced 3/4″ apart and 1/8″ deep.
2. Glue the ends to the back with the cross braces between them at top and bottom and all pieces even with the edges of the back.
3. Glue on the top.
4. Insert the shelves into the saw cuts.
5. "Books" can be made from strips of wood 7/16″ x 1 7/8″ x 1/2″. Make narrow grooves about 1/8″ or less apart to represent books. Color them with crayons.

Materials: Sofa

1 pc 3/4″ x 7/8″ x 3″—seat
1 pc 1/4″ x 1 1/2″ x 3 1/2″—back
2 pc 1/4″ x 1″ x 7/8″—arms

Construction:

1. Make a narrow saw cut or groove along the front (3/4″ side) of the seat 1/4″ from the upper edge.
2. Make two saw cuts 1″ apart and 1/4″ in depth to represent cushions.
3. Round off the upper corners of the back and upper front corners of the arms.
4. Glue the arms to the ends of the seat and add the back.

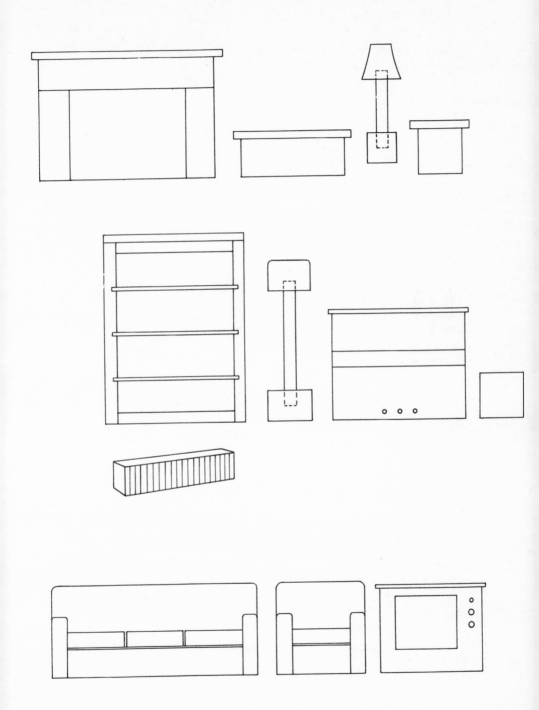

185

Materials: Chairs

2 pc 3/4" x 7/8" x 1"—seats
2 pc 1/4" x 1 1/2" x 1 1/2"—backs
4 pc 1/4" x 1" x 7/8"—arms

Construction:

1. Make a groove or narrow saw cut along the front (3/4" side) of the seat 1/4" from the upper edge.
2. Round off the upper corners of the backs and upper front corners of the arms.
3. Glue the arms to the ends of the seats and add the backs.

Materials: Tables

1 pc 3/4" x 1 3/4" x 5/8"—base ⎫
1 pc 1/8" x 1" x 2"—top ⎬ coffee table
3 pc 3/4" x 3/4" x 3/4"—bases ⎫
3 pc 1/8" x 1" x 1"—tops ⎬ end tables

Construction:

1. Glue the bases to the underside of the tops.

Materials: Piano and Bench

1 pc 3/4" x 2 1/4" x 1 3/4"—body section
1 pc 1/4" x 3/8" x 2 1/4"—keyboard section
1 pc 1/16" x 13/16" x 2 3/8"—top
2 colored pins—pedals
1 pc 3/4" x 3/4" x 3/4"—bench

Construction:

1. Glue the keyboard section to the body section 5/8" from upper edge, with 1/4" side against the front.
2. Glue on the top.
3. Install the pedals 1/8" from the lower edge and about 1/4" apart.

Materials: Television Set

1 pc 3/4" x 1 3/4" x 1 3/8"—cabinet
1 pc 1/16" x 13/16" x 1 7/8"—top
3 small brass nails or colored pins

Construction:

1. Glue the top piece to the cabinet even with the back edge. It will extend about 1/16" at each end and front.
2. Cut pieces about 1/4" long from the head end of the nails or pins and insert them into pilot holes made in the side of the cabinet about 1/4" apart.
3. Glue a small picture to the front of the cabinet for the screen. (colored picture if a color set)

Materials: Lamps

1 disk 1/2" x 3/4" in diameter—base
1—3/16" dowel 2" long—upright or shaft   } floor lamp
1 plastic bottle cap about 3/4" in diameter and 1/2" high-shade }
3 pc 1/2" dowel 1/2" long—base
3 pc 3/16" dowel 1 1/4" long—shaft } three table lamps
3 plastic tube caps—shades

Construction:

1. Drill a hole for the 3/16" dowel in the center of the base about 1/4" in depth.
2. Drive the shaft into the base.
3. Drill a 3/16" hole in the center of a small piece of wood and shape it to fit inside the cap. Insert the end of the dowel into this hole. Or, fill the tube cap with plastic wood. When partly hardened insert the dowel.

THE DINING ROOM

Materials: Table and Chairs

1 pc 1/8" x 1 1/2" x 3"—top
2 pc 1/2" x 3/4" x 1 1/8"—legs } table

6 pc 3/4" x 3/4" x 5/8"—bases
6 pc 1/8" x 3/4" x 13/16"—seats } chairs
6 pc 1/8" x 3/4" x 1 3/4"—backs

Construction:

1. Glue the legs to the underside of the table top 3/8" from the ends and side edges.
2. Glue the chair base to the back even with one end (lower).
3. Fasten on the seat which will extend 1/16" in front.

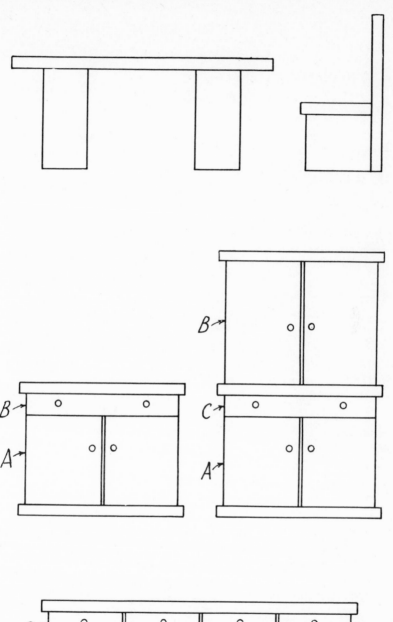

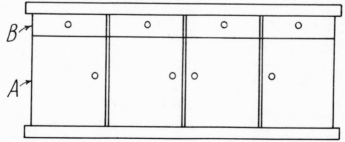

Materials: Server

1 pc 3/4" x 1 3/4" x 1"—A
1 pc 1/4" x 3/4" x 1 3/4"—B
2 pc 1/8" x 13/16" x 1 7/8"—top, base
4 colored pins—knobs

Construction:

1. Make a shallow vertical groove in the center of one side (front) of A for doors.
2. Glue B to top of A.
3. Glue on the top and the base. They will extend about 1/16" at the front and ends.
4. Drill holes for and drive in the pins.

Materials: China Cabinet

1 pc 3/4" x 1 3/4" x 1"—A
1 pc 3/4" x 1 3/4" x 1 3/8"—B
1 pc 1/4" x 3/4" x 1 3/4"—C
3 pc 1/8" x 13/16" x 1 7/8"—tops, base
6 colored pins—knobs

Construction:

1. Make a shallow vertical groove in the center of one side (front) of the A and B pieces to represent doors.
2. Glue the C piece to the top of the A piece even with the back edge of A.
3. Glue the top and base to the A piece and the top to the B piece. The tops and base will extend about 1/16" at the ends and front.
4. Glue the B section to the top of the A section even with the back edge of A and equidistant from the edges.
5. Drill holes for and drive in the pins.

Materials: Buffet

1 pc 3/4" x 3 1/2" x 1"—A
1 pc 1/4" x 3/4" x 3 1/2"—B
2 pc 1/8" x 13/16" x 3 5/8"—top, base
8 colored pins—knobs

Construction:

1. Glue piece B to one end of piece A (upper).
2. Make three shallow, vertical saw cuts in the front side of A and B 7/8" apart to represent doors and drawers.
3. Glue on the top and the base even with the back surface of A. These pieces will extend about 1/16" at the ends and front.
4. Drill pilot holes for and drive in the pins.

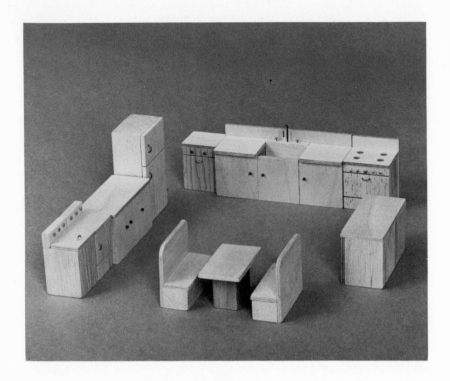

Materials: **Cabinet Sink and Cupboards**

2 pc 1 1/8" x 1 1/2" x 1 1/2"—A—end cupboards
1 pc 1 1/8" x 1" x 1 1/2"—B—sink cupboard
1 pc 1/4" x 5/8" x 1 1/2"—C—sink back
1 pc 1/8" x 4 1/2" x 2"—back
1 pc 1/8" x 4 1/2" x 1 1/2"—front
2 pc 1/8" x 1 3/8" x 1 1/2"—counter tops
2 large pins—for faucet handles
1 large paper clip—for spout
3 colored pins—for door knobs

Construction:

1. To make the sink and cupboard unit, glue the B piece between the two A pieces so that the grain in the A pieces is vertical while the grain in the B piece is horizontal. Arrange the pieces with the 1 1/2"

dimensions to the front or so the unit will be 4 1/2" long and 1 1/2" high. The lower side of the B piece should be even with the lower ends of the A pieces.

2. Glue the C piece to B between the end cupboards and even with one side (back) of the cupboards. Drill a small pilot hole in the center of C for the spout and a hole 3/8" on each side of the spout for the faucet handles.

3. Vertical grooves to represent doors about 1 1/2" apart can be made in the front piece with a fine saw, knife or pointed tool.

4. Glue the front and back to the unit even with the lower edges of A and B. Glue the counter tops in place on the A pieces.

5. Cut pieces about 1/4" long from the head ends of two pins for handles and insert them into the holes in the sink back.

6. Cut a piece about 1" long from the curved end of the paper clip for the spout and insert it into the center hole.

7. Cut pieces about 1/4" long from the head ends of the colored pins and insert them into pilot holes made in the doors about 1" from the lower edge of the front of the sink unit.

Materials: **Range**

2 pc 3/4" x 1 1/4" x 1 1/2"—A
1 pc 1/8" x 2" x 1 1/2"—back
1 pc 1/8" x 1 1/4" x 1 1/2"—top
4 common pins—burner controls
5 large pins (no. 24)—burners, oven control
2 paper clips (no. 1)—oven, broiler handles

Construction:

1. Glue the A pieces together to form a block 1 1/2" x 1 1/4" x 1 1/2" for the body of the range. The joint where the two pieces are glued together should be to the front of the range.

2. With a thin saw blade make cuts about 1/8" deep across the front of the block 3/8" and 1 1/4" from one end (lower). Also make vertical saw cuts along each side edge and bottom 1/8" in from the front of the range. These cuts will give the appearance of doors.

3. Drill pilot holes for the controls and handles as shown.

4. Drill four 1/4" holes in the top piece 3/8" in from the ends and front and back edges.

5. Glue the back and top in place.

6. In the center of each 1/4" hole in the top drill a pilot hole for

the burner. Cut four pieces about 3/8" long from the head ends of the large pins and drive them into these holes so that the heads are about even with the top of the range.

7. Cut pieces about 1/4" long from the common pins and the curved ends of the paper clips and drive them into the holes drilled for the burner controls and door handles.

Materials: **Refrigerator**

1 pc 1 1/8" x 1 3/4" x 3"
2 paper clips—handles

Construction:

1. Make a cut with a fine saw blade across the front 1" from the top. Also make saw cuts about 1/16" deep and 1/8" from the edges along the sides and ends of the block to represent doors.

2. Drill holes for and install the paper clip handles about 3/8" down from the top of each door and 1/4" from the side edge.

Materials: **Washer and Dryer**

2 pc 1 1/8" x 1 1/4" x 1 1/2"
2 pc 1/4" x 1/2" x 1 1/4"—for control panel
2 pc 1/8" x 15/16" x 1 1/4"—tops
6 large pins—controls
2 paper clips—handles

Construction:

1. Make a narrow saw cut across the front of one block 1/2" from one end (lower). This will be the dryer.

2. Drill holes for the handle about 3/8" down from the top and 1/4" from one edge.

3. Drill three holes in each control panel, one in the center and one 1/4" from each end. Locate the holes 1/8" from upper edge. Install the controls.

4. Glue the control section to the top of each block even with the back of the blocks.

5. Glue on the tops.

6. Drill holes for the handle in the washer 1/4" from the front edge.

7. Install the handles in both appliances.

Materials: Dishwasher

1 pc 1 1/8" x 1 1/4" x 1 1/2"
1 pc 1/8" x 1 1/8" x 1 1/4"—top
2 large pins—controls
1 paper clip—door handle

Construction:

1. Make a narrow groove across one side (front) 1/4" from one end (upper). Also make grooves 1/8" in from the side edges and lower end to represent the door.
2. Drill pilot holes for and drive the pieces cut from pins into the upper part of the front for the controls.
3. Drill holes 1/4" apart for the paper clip handle.
4. Glue on the top.

Materials: Two Cupboards

2 pc 1 1/8" x 3" x 1 1/2"
2 pc 1/8" x 3" x 1 1/2"—fronts
2 pc 1/8" x 1 5/16" x 3"—tops
6 colored pins—knobs

Construction:

1. Glue on the fronts. Make vertical saw cuts in the front pieces 1" apart to represent doors.
2. Glue on the tops which will extend about 1/16" in front.
3. Drill holes for and drive in the knobs.

Materials: Table and Benches

1 pc 3/4" x 1 1/4" x 1 1/8"—base ⎱
1 pc 1/8" x 1 1/4" x 2 1/4"—top ⎰ table
2 pc 3/4" x 5/8" x 2 1/4"—A ⎱
2 pc 1/8" x 13/16" x 2 1/4"—B ⎰ seats
2 pc 1/8" x 1 7/8" x 2 1/4"—backs

Construction:

1. Center the base on the underside of the table top and glue.
2. Round off two corners (upper) of each bench back.
3. Glue the A pieces to the backs even with the lower edges. Glue the B pieces to the upper side of the A pieces.

Materials: Twin Beds

2 pc 3/4" x 1 5/8" x 3"—A—springs and mattresses
2 pc 1/8" x 1 3/4" x 1 5/8"—headboards
2 pc 1/8" x 1 1/4" x 1 5/8"—footboards

Construction:

1. With a thin saw blade make a shallow groove along each 3/4"
side of the A pieces midway between the edges.

2. Round off two corners (upper) of the headboards and footboards.
Draw a light line 1/4" from the lower edge of each board. Using the
lines as guides, glue the boards to the ends of A. The springs will be
1/4" off the floor.

Materials: **Dresser**

1 pc 7/8" x 1 3/4" x 2 1/4"—body
2 pc 1/8" x 7/8" x 1 3/4"—ends
1 pc 1/8" x 7/8" x 2 1/2"—base
1 pc 1/8" x 15/16" x 2 5/8"—top
10 colored pins

Materials: **Chest of Drawers**

1 pc 7/8" x 1 7/8" x 1 1/2"—body
2 pc 1/8" x 7/8" x 1 7/8"—ends
1 pc 1/8" x 7/8" x 1 3/4"—base
1 pc 1/8" x 15/16" x 1 7/8"—top
10 colored pins

Construction:

1. Make narrow grooves in the front of each body piece about 5/16" apart to represent drawers. The top drawers may be made narrower and the bottom drawers wider.
2. Assemble the dresser and chest of drawers by gluing on the ends, the bases and the tops. The tops will extend a little at the ends and front.
3. Drill pilot holes for and drive in the pins 3/8" in from the ends of each drawer of the dresser, and 1/4" for the chest.

Materials: **Dressing Table**

2 pc 3/4" x 7/8" x 1 1/4"—pedestals
1 pc 1/4" x 7/8" x 1"—center drawer
1 pc 1/8" x 15/16" x 2 5/8"—top
9 colored pins

Construction:

1. In the front (3/4" side) of each pedestal make narrow grooves to represent drawers. Make the top two drawers in each pedestal about 1/4" wide and the lower two 3/8" wide.
2. Glue the center drawer to the underside of the top even with the back edge and centered.
3. Glue the pedestals to the top even with the back edge and against the ends of the center drawer.
4. Drill pilot holes for and drive in the pins.

Materials: **Chairs**

3 pc 3/4" x 3/4" x 5/8"—bases
3 pc 1/8" x 3/4" x 1 1/2"—backs
3 pc 1/8" x 3/4" x 13/16"—seats

Construction:

1. Glue the back to the base even with the lower end and add the seat.

Materials: **Lamps**

2 pc 3/8" dowel 1/2" long—bases
2 large furniture nails—shades

Construction:

1. Drill a pilot hole in the center of each lamp base and drive the furniture nail part way in leaving a space about 1/4" wide between the shade and base.

Materials: **Night Table**

1 pc 3/4" x 3/4" x 3/4"—base
1 pc 1/8" x 1" x 1"—top

Construction:

1. Center the base on the underside of the top and glue in place.

THE CHILDREN'S ROOM

Materials: **Cribs**

2 pc 1/4" x 1 1/4" x 2"—bottoms
4 pc 1/8" x 2" x 1 1/2"—ends
4 pc 1/8" x 1" x 2"—sides

Construction:

1. Round off two corners (upper) of each end.
2. Glue the bottom between the ends 1/2" from the lower edge.
3. Glue the sides to the bottom and ends.

Materials: **Chests of Drawers**

2 pc 1 1/8" x 1 3/4" x 1 1/2"—body
2 pc 1/8" x 1 3/16" x 1 3/4"—bases
2 pc 1/8" x 1 3/16" x 1 3/4"—tops
16 colored pins—knobs

Construction:

1. Make narrow grooves in the front of the body about 3/8″ apart to represent drawers.
2. Glue on the base and the top. Both will extend a little in the front.
3. Drill holes for and insert the pins 5/16″ in from the ends of each drawer.

Materials: Chairs

2 pc 3/4″ x 3/4″ x 5/8″—base
2 pc 1/8″ x 3/4″ x 1 1/2″—back
2 pc 1/8″ x 3/4″ x 13/16″—seat

Construction:

1. Glue the back to the base even with the lower end and add the seat.

Materials: Lamps

2 pc 1/4″ dowel 3/8″ long—bases
2—3/16″ ferrules
2 brass furniture nails about 5/16″ in diameter

Construction:

1. Drill a pilot hole for the nails in the center of each dowel.
2. Insert the nail through the ferrule into the dowel.

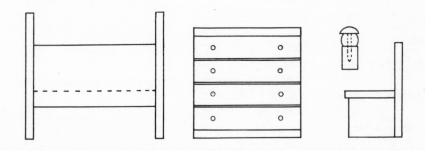

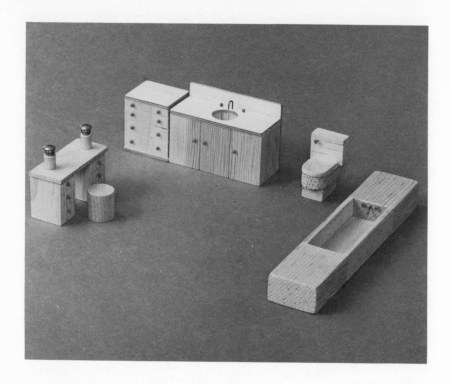

Materials: **Cabinet Lavatory**

1 pc 1 1/8" x 3" x 1 1/2"—A
1 pc 1/8" x 1 3/16" x 3"—top
1 pc 1/8" x 2" x 3"—back
5 colored pins—faucet handles—knobs
1 paper clip—spout

Construction:

1. In one side (front) of the A piece make two narrow vertical grooves with the grain of the wood 1" apart.

2. Glue the back on even with the lower end of A. Glue on the top.

3. In the center of the top drill a 3/4" hole about 3/8" deep 9/16" from the front edge for the basin.

4. Cut a 1/2" piece from the curved end of the paper clip for the

spout. Drill a pilot hole for the spout at the back of the basin and centered. Drill pilot holes for the faucet handles 3/8" to either side of the
spout and for the door knobs in the front of the cabinet about 5/8"
down from the top. Install the spout, handles and knobs.

Materials: Toilet

1 pc 7/16" x 3/4" x 1 1/2"—bowl
1 pc 1/8" x 3/4" x 1"—cover
1 pc 7/16" x 5/8" x 1"—base
1 pc 7/16" x 3/4" x 1"—water tank
1 large pin—for lever

Construction:

1. Glue the cover to one end (front) of the bowl even with the
end. Round off the ends of the two pieces.
2. Center the base on the underside of the bowl and glue.
3. Drive the flush lever into the front of the tank and glue the tank
to the top of the bowl against the back end of the cover.

Materials: Built-in Bathtub

1 pc 1/4" x 1" x 3"—bottom
2 pc 3/16" x 3/4" x 3"—sides
2 pc 3/4" x 1 3/8" x 2"—end sections
2 large pins—for faucet handles
1 paper clip—for spout

Construction:

1. Glue the sides to the bottom even with the underside of the bottom.
2. Drill pilot holes for and install the spout and faucet handles in
one end section.
3. Glue the end sections to the sides and bottom of the tub.

Materials: Dressing Table and Stool

2 pc 3/4" x 1" x 1 1/4"—pedestals
1 pc 1/8" x 1 1/16" x 2 1/2"—top
6 colored pins—for knobs
1 pc 3/4" dowel 3/4" long—stool

Construction:

1. Make two narrow grooves in the 3/4″ side (front) of each pedestal 3/8″ from the top and 3/8″ apart to represent drawers.

2. Glue the pedestals to the underside of the top even with the back edge and about 1/16″ in from the ends of the top. The top will extend about 1/16″ at the front.

3. Drill pilot holes for and drive in the knobs.

Materials: **Chest of Drawers**

1 pc 1 1/8″ x 1 1/2″ x 1 1/2″—body
1 pc 1/8″ x 1 5/16″ x 1 1/2″—top
1 pc 1/8″ x 1 1/2″ x 1 1/2″—front
1 pc 1/8″ x 1 5/16″ x 1 1/2″—base
8 colored pins—for knobs

Construction:

1. In the front piece make three narrow horizontal grooves to represent drawers. Locate the first groove 1/4″ from the upper end of the body and space the other two 3/8″ apart.

2. Glue the front, top and base to the body. The top and base will extend about 1/16″ at the front.

3. Drill pilot holes about 1/4″ in from the side edges for the knobs and drive them in.

Materials: **Lamps**

2 pc 3/8″ dowel 1/2″ long—base
2 large furniture nails—shades

Construction:

1. In the center of the dowel base drill a pilot hole for the nail. Drive the nail part way into the hole leaving a space about 1/4″ in width between the shade and the base.

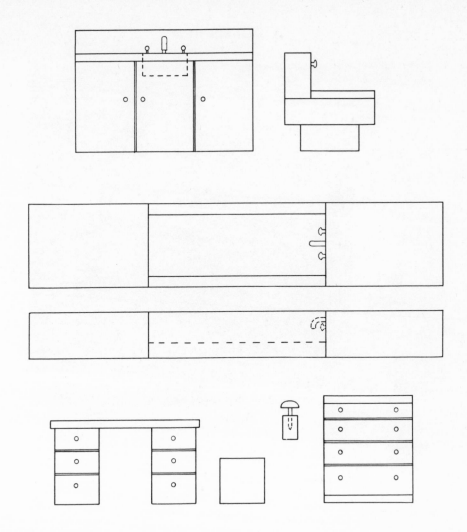

A DOLL'S BED

Materials:

8 pc 3/4″ x 1 1/2″ x 10″—A ⎫
4 pc 7/16″ x 1 1/2″ x 4″—B ⎬ legs
4 pc 7/16″ x 1 1/2″ x 2 1/2″—C ⎭
2 pc 7/16″ x 3 1/2″ x 22″—sides
2 pc 3/4″ x 5 1/2″ x 8″—headboard, footboard
2 pc 7/16″ x 1/2″ x 18 3/4″—bottom supports
1 pc 1/4″ plywood 9 1/2″ x 18 3/4″—bottom
12—2″ no. 6 flat head screws
8—1 1/2″ no. 6 flat head screws
6—3/4″ no. 6 flat head screws

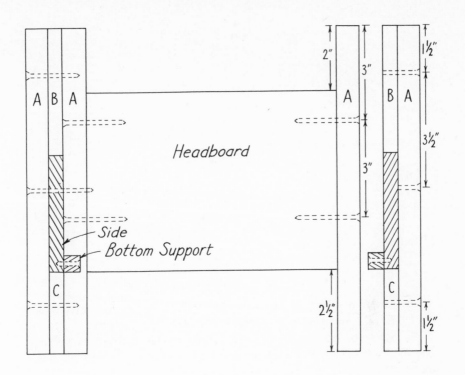

A | B | A

Headboard

Side

Bottom Support

C

2"

3"

3"

2½"

1½"

3½"

1½"

A | B | A

C

Construction:

1. Sand one 1 1/2" side, which will be the outside, of each A piece.

2. To each A piece glue a B piece to the side not sanded and even with one end (upper).

3. Lay two of these assemblies on the bench and glue a side piece to the A pieces and against the ends of the B pieces. The end of the side piece should be even with the edges of A and B.

4. Glue a C piece to each A piece with one end of C against the edge of the side. Make the other side the same way.

5. In the A pieces used so far drill and countersink holes for screws 1 1/2" from each end and 5" from the upper end and centered between the side edges.

6. In each of the four remaining A pieces drill and countersink holes for screws 3" and 6" from one end (upper) and centered. Drill from the side not sanded. Fasten the ends of the headboard and footboard to the sanded sides of these four A pieces 2 1/2" from the lower end and centered. Use glue and 2" screws.

7. In each bottom support drill and countersink three holes for screws 2" from either end and at the center.

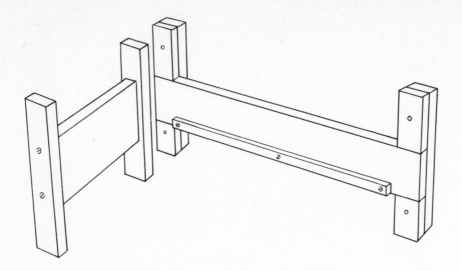

8. Fasten the supports to the inside surface of the sides even with the lower edge and 1 5/8" from either end. Use 3/4" screws.

9. Screw the side assemblies to the headboard and footboard assemblies. Use the remaining four 2" screws in the holes in the A pieces 5" from the upper end and the 1 1/2" screws in the other eight holes.

10. Put in the bottom board which will lie on the side supports.

11. Varnish, stain or paint the bed. Decals may be used to decorate it.

A SWINGING CRADLE

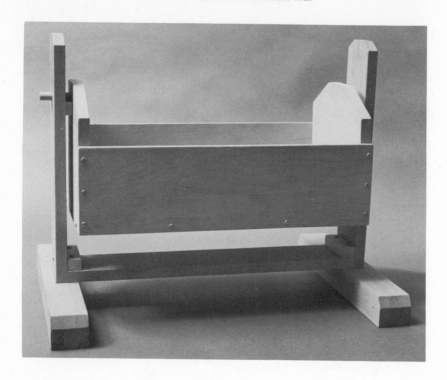

Materials:

2 pc 3/4" x 8 3/4" x 9"—ends ⎤
1 pc 3/4" x 9" x 18 1/2"—bottom ⎬ cradle
2 pc 7/16" x 5 1/2" x 20"—sides ⎦
2 pc 3/4" x 3 1/2" x 18"—upright posts
4 pc 3/4" x 2" x 16"—A ⎤
4 pc 3/4" x 2" x 6 1/4"—B ⎦ feet
1 pc 3/4" x 3 1/2" x 21"—brace
2 pc 3/4" x 1" x 3 1/2"—C
2 pc 1/2" x 3/4" x 3"—D
2 pc 1/2" dowel 2 1/2" long
4—1 1/4" no. 6 flat head screws
8—1 1/2" no. 6 flat head screws
4—2" no. 6 flat head screws
16—1" no. 6 pan head or round head screws
6—no. 6 finishing nails

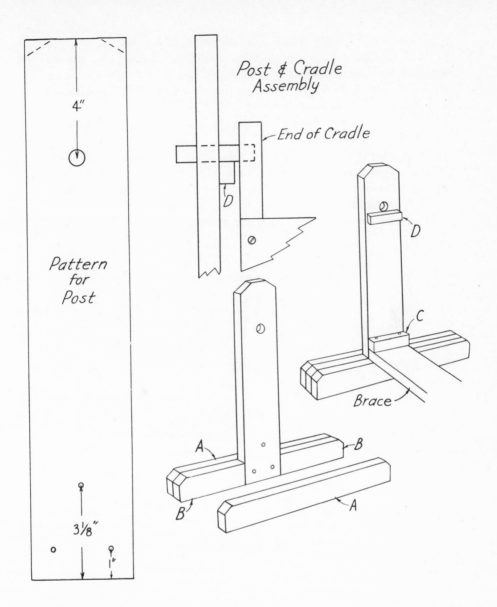

Pattern for Post

4"

3⅛"

1"

Post & Cradle Assembly

End of Cradle

D

D

C

Brace

A

B

B

A

Construction:

1. To make the end pieces as shown in the diagram set the miter gauge at 60 degrees. Along one 9" edge measure in 3" and make cut 1. When making this cut fasten the stop to the miter gauge so that the lower end of the piece is against the stop. Turn the piece over and make cut 2. Or, the ends may be shaped as shown by dotted line in the diagram. A 12" plate can be used to draw the curve.

2. Drill a 1/2″ hole about 1/2″ in depth in one side of each end 1″ from the upper edge and centered. Along the bottom edge on the same side drill and countersink three holes for 1 1/2″ screws. Locate them 3/8″ from the edge, 1″ from either side with one midway between these two.

3. Glue and screw the ends to the bottom with the 1/2″ holes to the outside.

4. In each side piece drill holes for eight pan or round head screws 3/8″ from the edges. The end holes are 3/4″ from the top and bottom edges with one midway between them. The two along the lower edges are 6″ from the ends.

5. Fasten the sides to the ends and bottom.

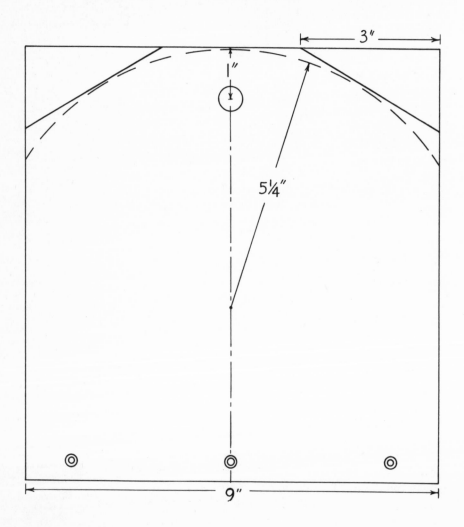

6. With the miter gauge set at 60 degrees saw off the corners of one end (top) of each post and two corners (upper) of each A and B piece. Be sure that all saw cuts on the A and B pieces are the same so that they will fit together correctly. If the ends of the cradle are curved, make the ends of the posts and A and B pieces also curved.

7. In each end post, drill a hole slightly larger than 1/2", 4" from the upper end and centered. Also drill and countersink a hole for a screw 3 1/8" from the lower end and centered. Drill two holes 3/4" from the side edges and 1" from the lower end for 1 1/4" screws. Glue a D piece to the inside surface of each post just below the hole for the dowel.

8. To make the post assemblies glue a B piece to an A piece, then the post and another B piece. Make sure that all parts are even at the ends and lower edges. Drive two 1 1/4" screws through the post into the A piece. Glue and nail on another A piece to complete the assembly.

9. Glue the C pieces to the brace even with the ends of the brace and with the 1" surface down. Drill and countersink two holes for screws through each C piece and the brace, locating them 3/8" from the brace end and 3/4" in from the ends of the C pieces.

10. Glue and screw the brace to the inside A pieces between the posts using 2" screws.

11. Drive a 1 1/2" screw through the hole in each post into C.

12. Varnish, stain or paint the cradle. Decorate it with decals, if desired.

13. To hang the cradle between the posts, put glue in the 1/2" holes in the ends. Wax the dowels except the end to be glued. Hold the cradle in position between the posts and insert the dowels through the posts into the holes in the ends of the cradle.

A GAMBREL ROOF BARN

Materials:

2 pc 3/4" x 10" x 12"—ends

1 pc 3/4" x 10" x 14 1/2"—floor

2 pc 3/4" x 2" x 14 1/2"—front, rear braces

2 pc 3/4" x 2" x 14 1/2"—ridge brace

2 pc 1/4" x 5 1/2" x 6 5/8"—front ⎫
1 pc 1/4" x 16" x 1 1/2"—rear ⎬ sides

1 pc 1/4" x 5" x 3/4"—A ⎫
1 pc 1/4" x 5" x 1 1/2"—B ⎬ filler

2 pc 1/4" x 3 3/4" x 16 1/2"—C—lower ⎫
2 pc 1/4" x 5" x 16 1/2"—D—upper ⎬ roof

2 pc 1/4" x 2 3/4" x 5"—doors

1 pc 1/2" x 5/8" x 11"—track—upper

1 pc 1/2" x 3/4" x 11"—track—lower

4—1/2" no. 6 pan head screws—handles, stops

18—2" no. 6 flat head screws

No. 18—1 1/4" brads

No. 18—3/4" brads

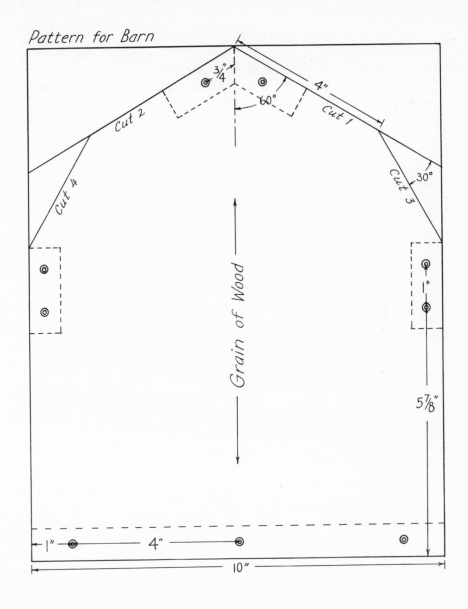

Pattern for Barn

Cut 2

Cut 4

3/4"

60°

Cut 1

4"

Cut 3

30°

Grain of Wood

5⅞"

1"

1"

4"

10"

Construction:

1. Mark the center of the top 3/4″ surface of the 10″ edge of each end section, and draw a line across using the try square as a guide.

2. Set the miter gauge at 60 degrees and, with the stop on the miter gauge against the lower end of the piece, make cut 1 starting at this line. Then, turn the piece over and make cut 2. Make the other end section the same way.

3. Along the upper slope, just cut, measure down 4″ from the peak and, again using the try square as a guide, draw a line across the edge.

4. Set the gauge at 30 degrees. Move the stop so that it is again against the lower end of the piece and make cut 3. Turn the piece over and make cut 4. Do the same for the other end section.

5. In each end piece drill and countersink 9 holes for screws 3/8″ from the edges in locations as shown. See diagram.

6. Glue and screw the ends to the floor. Install the front and rear braces between the ends. The upper outside corners of each brace should be even with the lower angle of the end pieces.

7. Saw one side edge of each ridge brace with the saw tilted at 30 degrees. Glue these two edges together to form an angle which will be the same as the angle of the ends. Fasten the brace in place between the ends.

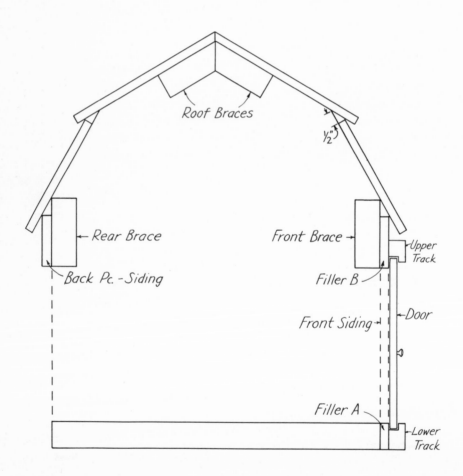

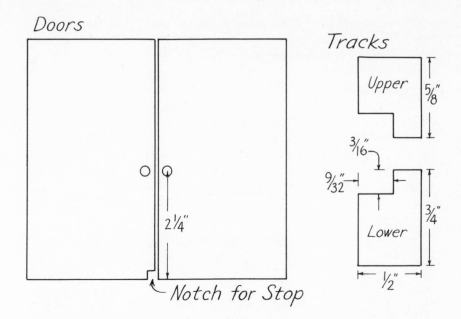

Doors

Tracks

Upper $5/_8''$

$3/_{16}''$

$9/_{32}''$ Lower $3/_4''$

$2 1/_4''$

Notch for Stop

$1/_2''$

8. Nail on the two front pieces of siding even with the bottom edge of the floor leaving a 5" wide opening at the center of the barn. When fastening the siding to the front brace use the 3/4" brads.

9. In the 5" opening glue filler piece A against the edge of the floor between the siding. Glue piece B to the brace even with the lower edge of the brace.

10. Along the lower slopes of the ends of the barn measure down 1/2" and draw a line across. Use try square as a guide. Nail the C roof pieces to the ends with the upper edge on the lines.

11. Tilt the saw at 30 degrees. With the underside of each D piece up, saw a narrow strip lengthwise off each piece. When the roof pieces meet at the peak with the right side up they will conform to the same angles as the ridge brace and ends of the barn. The brads should be in 5/8" from the ends of the roof pieces; one brad 1 1/4" from the lower edges and the other 1/2" from the upper edges. The roof boards will extend 1/4" at each end. Use 3/4" brads when nailing roof to the ridge brace.

12. Using 3/4" brads nail the back piece of siding to the ends and brace.

13. In each piece for the track, make a groove for the doors to slide in by cutting a rabbet about 3/16" in depth and a little over 1/4" wide.

14. Glue and nail the lower track to the barn 2 1/2" from each end and even with the lower edge of the siding.

15. Set the doors temporarily in place to locate the upper track

which will be about 4 5/8″ above the lower track. Glue and nail the upper track to the barn.

16. Drill a pilot hole for the handles and screw them into the doors 2 1/4″ from the lower end and 1/4″ from one edge.

17. In the lower front edge of one door make a small notch. Drive a brad through the lower track near the center so that the notch will strike the nail. The doors will then stop at the center when they are closed. If the barn is to be painted do it before installing the doors.

18. Slide the doors into the tracks and screw in a stop 1/8″ beyond each end of the lower track and up 1/2″ from the lower edge of the front.